THE ERA OF EXPANSION: 1800–1848

AMERICAN REPUBLIC SERIES

EDITED BY DON E. FEHRENBACHER AND OTIS A. PEASE

THE ERA OF
EXPANSION: 1800–1848

DON E. FEHRENBACHER
Stanford University

John Wiley & Sons, Inc.
NEW YORK · LONDON · SYDNEY · TORONTO

To Stockton and VeNona Swaney

Library of Congress Catalog Card Number: 68-8713
Cloth: SBN 471 25690 0   Paper: SBN 471 25691 9
Printed in the United States of America

Preface

Viewed across more than a century of accelerating change, Jeffersonian and Jacksonian America may seem not only remote but largely irrelevant. In temper as well as circumstances, we are far removed from the day of the mountain man and the pioneer farmer, from the Embargo and the Bank War, from the Gold Rush and the fall of the Alamo, from that springtime of national pride when Joel Barlow proclaimed that in this new world, "social man a second birth shall find." It is difficult now to recapture the sense of throbbing potentiality and the expansive optimism of a young nation that half believed itself marked by destiny for a special role in history. Yet, to a striking degree, the United States and its people still move in cultural grooves that were cut during the first half of the nineteenth century. There one must look for the shaping of our political party system, for the foundations of modern judicial power, and for the origins of our corporate structure and industrial technology. There also are the beginnings of organized social reform, the opening phases of the struggle for racial equality, the first awakening to the problem of urban poverty, and the first instance of widespread moral protest against a foreign war. In addition, that was our national adolescence, an age of prodigious physical growth, when the Republic doubled and very nearly redoubled its original size and expanded westward at such a rapid pace that only forty-seven years intervened between the admission of Ohio and the admission of California as states of the Union. Virtually every other segment of American life, from the functioning of the slavery system to the writing of lyric poetry, was in some way affected by the elemental force of the advance across the continent.

The Era of Expansion is one of seven volumes in the "Wiley American Republic Series," a joint effort at exploring the meaning of the past to the present. Each of these books is a self-contained study by a specialist in the period treated. Together, they cover the whole chronological range of American history. Designed to be illuminating rather than comprehensive, the Series limits its presentation of factual details in order to make room for fuller explanation of major events and trends. Recognizing, moreover, that the record of the past continually changes as historical data are screened through the minds of different historians, each author in the Series concludes his volume with an extensive historiographical essay, an effective reminder that no one can have the last word on the subject.

Don E. Fehrenbacher
Otis A. Pease

Contents

List of Maps

(*Maps and charts by John V. Morris*)

Chapter I

Introduction

From Berlin, on November 25, 1800, the young diplomat sent home another long letter. "I hope and confidently believe," he wrote, "that you will be prepared to bear this event with calmness and composure, if not with indifference; that you will not suffer it to prey upon your mind, or affect your health; nor even to think more hardly of your country than she deserves." Thus John Quincy Adams consoled his father after learning the results of the presidential election. Twenty-eight years later, he would experience the same bitter defeat and retire with the same stoical pride. The passionate love of both men for their country was seldom returned in equal measure by a populace that saw only the sterner side of their natures.

Although recalled in 1801 from his post as minister to Prussia, the younger Adams was just beginning a public career that would extend almost continuously over more than half a century. Successively Senator, Minister to Russia and Great Britain, Secretary of State, and President, he then added nearly two decades of service as Congressman from Massachusetts. At the age of eighty, John Quincy Adams collapsed in the House of Representatives and died there on February 23, 1848. His life, begun in the year of the Townshend Acts, ended with gold already discovered in California. He was present with his father in 1783 when the Treaty of Paris confirmed the birth of a new nation; three weeks before his death, the Treaty of Guadalupe Hidalgo completed that nation's expansion to the Pacific Ocean. He had been appointed to his first office by George Washington, and one member of the committee named to make arrangements for his funeral was Abraham Lincoln. "My stern chase after Time," he wrote near the end, "is like the race of a man with a wooden leg after a horse." Time had been full of change during the years of his pursuit. The country that he left behind was in countless ways vastly different from the one to which he had given his youthful allegiance.

The United States in 1800 extended westward only to the Mississippi River. Bounded on three sides by colonial territory of European powers, it covered less than a million square miles, and much of this domain was still wilderness. Just two states had emerged west of the Appalachians, and vast areas remained in the possession of Indian tribes that were capable of fierce resistance to encroachment. By 1848, virtually the entire region had achieved statehood, and most of the Indians were gone—either annihilated or forcibly removed to the Western plains. The nation, meanwhile, had more than tripled its original size, expanding southward to the Gulf of Mexico and the Rio Grande, sweeping westward to the shores of Oregon and California. Within a lifetime, thirteen Atlantic colonies had become a transcontinental republic.

There were multiple forces behind the thrust of national expansion. The desire for military security and for commercial advantage spurred efforts to acquire strategically important spots like the mouth of the Mississippi. An aggressive faith in the transcendent destiny of the United States fortified official policy. But the primary impulse came from the restless individual energies of the people themselves. Westward migration increased rapidly during the early nineteenth century. A flood of settlers poured into the Mississippi Valley, and from there smaller streams continued on toward more distant parts of the continent. American traders and pioneers preceded American sovereignty into Louisiana, Texas, Utah, Oregon, and California. Each wagon rolling westward was an instrument of conquest and an appropriate symbol for the era of expansion.

The territory added to the United States between 1803 and 1848 was acquired by diplomacy, by military conquest, and by combinations of the two. Twice during the period, Americans found themselves at war. Expansionist feeling helped precipitate hostilities with Britain in 1812, though the most pervasive influence was the determination of a young nation to defend its sovereign rights. The Mexican War from 1846 to 1848 was more plainly a war of expansion, and one that ended in heady success. Both conflicts were major turning points in American history. After the Treaty of Ghent, which coincided with the restoration of peace in Europe, national interest shifted from external threats to challenging domestic problems and opportunities. The War of 1812 was the last war in which foreign armies invaded

American soil, and the nation settled back behind its ocean ramparts to a security not to be breached until the age of nuclear power. The victory over Mexico culminated and virtually ended continental expansion. By reviving the issue of slavery in the territories, it inaugurated the decisive phase of the sectional controversy and set the Republic on a precipitous course to disaster.

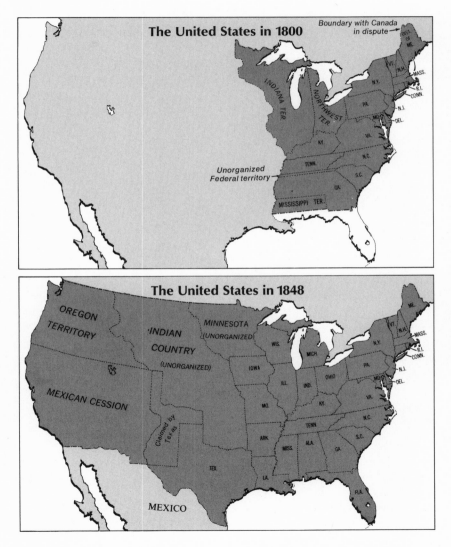

Territorial expansion drew off large numbers of people from the Eastern seaboard. By 1850, two million white Americans who had been born in Atlantic coastal states were living farther west, whereas only about 50,000 natives of the West had moved to the East. Despite this drain, however, the population of the Atlantic states more than doubled during the first half of the century, and that of the Republic as a whole rose from 5 million to 23 million. At first, natural increase accounted for nearly all of the population growth. Then a decline in the birth rate set in, but it was counterbalanced by the onset of mass immigration. As a consequence, the increase of total population by decades remained virtually uniform, never varying appreciably from 35 percent. However, the great influx of immigrants from Ireland, Germany, and other European countries produced significant changes in the composition and character of the American nation. There were 370,000 new arrivals in the year 1850 alone, by which time nearly one-tenth of the entire population was foreign-born.

Slower to gather momentum than the westward movement and immigration, but full of meaning for the future, was the progress of urbanization. Cities of ten thousand people or more held only about 3.5 percent of the population in 1800 and 11 percent in 1850, but they were places where leadership, wealth, and creative energy tended to concentrate, where major decisions were made, and where new projects were conceived. In the West as well as the East, and even in the South, the social power of the city greatly exceeded the numerical strength of its population. The urban environment posed problems that an individualistic and rural-minded people could not easily solve, but by mid-century many Americans had become aware that the city was in some respects another kind of wilderness to tame.

Urbanization, like many other social trends of the era, was bound up with the sweep of economic change. These were the seminal years of the industrial revolution in America. John Quincy Adams lived to see the shape of the future as the nation entered its period of transition from a preindustrial to an industrial order. By 1848, improvements in transportation had facilitated the development of a national market system. The rise of the great cotton kingdom was the most spectacular aspect of a general shift from subsistence to commercial agriculture. The techniques of mass production, already well established in the manufacture of textiles, were gradually spreading to other industries, and the craftsman was learning that he could not compete with power-driven machinery. Labor unions had made their appearance. Banking had become a major enterprise, responding with promiscuous energy to the expansive need for credit and instruments of commercial exchange. Corporate organization was growing in popularity as a means of raising large amounts of capital. Furthermore, the passion for business and profits—the determination to get ahead—had quickened the tempo of life at nearly every social level. The "almighty dollar," Washington Irving observed in the 1850s, had become the "great object of universal devotion" throughout the country.

According to some European visitors, the American people were preoccupied with business conditions, crop prices, and land sales. Others said that the chief interest was in parties, candidates, and elections. The difference may have been largely a matter of timing; for economic affairs were a daily concern and subject to unpredictable fluctuations, whereas political excitement rose and subsided with regular campaign cycles. Elections occurred so frequently, however, and on such a variety of schedules throughout the country, that the traveler seldom failed to find one or more in progress. By the Jacksonian period, in any case, the widespread popular enthusiasm that animated politics was a distinctive feature of American life.

The first two political parties had grown out of a split in Washington's administration over important national issues. Competition for the presidency then developed as a consequence. Federalism triumphed in 1796, but met defeat four years later and began to wither away. By 1820, the Jeffersonian Republicans had no organized opposition. Such unity was unnatural in American politics, however, and it soon disappeared. An interval of factional struggles was followed by a revival of the two-party system, but in somewhat different circumstances. This time, the process began with the contest for the presidency, which produced coalitions that evolved into the Democratic and Whig parties.

By the 1830s, politics and especially presidential politics had become more dramatic and more democratic. Presidential electors were now generally chosen by the voters instead of the state legislatures. The convention system, just coming into use as a means of nominating party candidates, was not only another step toward democracy but also a splendid innovation that seemed to concentrate all the excitement of politics in one public spectacle. Meanwhile, a trend toward universal suffrage had expanded the electorate in many states, and partisan newspapers, multiplying at a remarkable rate, kept the air saturated with political argument. Closely associated with the growth of popular interest and participation in politics was the emergence of a campaign style so full of noisy enthusiasm and dramatic appeal that it became in itself an important cultural expression.

The spirit of democracy acquired its supreme symbol with the election of Andrew Jackson, who demonstrated that popular appeal could outweigh other advantages in the contest for political power. Jackson's image as the perfect democrat emanated principally from his Western background. The tendency to associate democratic ideals with frontier characteristics became a significant factor in national politics. Its most prominent beneficiary would be Abraham Lincoln. But Jackson, of course, had a second and greater claim upon the affection of the public; for he was a military hero—the scourge of the Creeks and the victor of New Orleans. The American nation, lacking a historical tradition that extended back into the distant past, had to fashion its myths from contemporary materials. It needed heroes as a basis for national legend, and heroic reputations were usually made on the battlefield. After Jackson's success, there was a parade of military figures to the forefront of American politics.

The election of Jackson in 1828 was also the pivotal event in the restoration of the two-party system. While he and his followers were building a formidable political machine, anti-Jackson elements gradually combined to form an effective opposition. By the 1840s the Whig and Democratic parties were well organized, evenly matched, regionally balanced, and equally committed to the democratic style in politics. The exceedingly close presidential elections of this decade added more excitement to the political scene. Both parties wrestled constantly with the problem of maintaining unity while recruiting adherents in all sections of the country and at all levels of society. Consequently, there was a tendency to evade or muffle the troublesome issues confronting the country and to concentrate upon the business of winning elections as an end in itself. The political party had become something more than a vehicle of popular opinion. It was an active agency with its own intrinsic purposes to follow and interests to protect.

The intense rivalry between Whigs and Democrats had an artificial quality because it did not reflect the growing sectional cleavage in the country, which manifested itself primarily *within* the two parties. Each could survive as a national organization only by avoiding the most dangerous issue and concealing with rhetoric its internal discord. Nothing better demonstrated the separation of party politics from political realities than the presidential election of 1848. The results of that contest reflected no sectional pattern. The Whigs and Democrats showed about equal strength in both the North and the South. Yet, at this very time, a sectional crisis of major proportions was developing over the status of slavery in the newly acquired Mexican

Cession. Thus, whereas political allegiance served as a bond of national unity, neither party could deal effectively with the one problem that seriously threatened national unity. And the forces that would ultimately disrupt the Union were already undermining this second two-party system.

Although national politics aroused the greatest public interest, daily life in America was much more affected by what happened at the state and local levels. The state government and its subsidiaries determined who could vote, regulated and promoted business enterprise, built schools and roads, provided protection against crime and fire, and set the rules governing marriage and divorce, partnership and incorporation, inheritance, transfer of property, bankruptcy, professional practice, apprenticeship, and slavery. The significant changes in the structure and function of government were occurring principally within the separate states. The federal government, in comparison, remained more or less static throughout the first half of the nineteenth century.

The chief activities of the federal government in 1850 were about the same as in 1800. They included national defense, the conduct of foreign relations, regulation of Indian affairs, sale of public lands, postal service, and collection of import duties. No important new function had been added to the list, and indeed the government had withdrawn from the field of banking. Outside the post office system, there were fewer than 5000 civilian federal employees in the whole country, and annual federal expenditures amounted to only $1.70 per capita.

In an era when most of the states were rewriting their constitutions, the fundamental law of the Republic underwent no formal alteration. Between 1804 and 1865 not a single amendment was added to the Federal Constitution. To be sure, considerable change did occur as a result of interpretation. The growing influence of the Supreme Court, for example, which firmly established its right to overrule state courts and invalidate state legislation, significantly affected the structure of the federal system. At the same time, the Court under John Marshall's leadership broadened the scope of federal power, endorsing the principle of "loose construction" and interpreting the commerce clause in expansive terms. But since stricter constitutional views tended to prevail in Congress and the presidency, the activities of the government seldom approached the limits of its authority. Consequently, not until 1857 did the Supreme Court nullify any major piece of federal legislation, and the ideal of the negative state seemed to be most honored in the nation's capital.

The federal Constitution thus represented continuity and stability in a changing nation. Regarded essentially as an instrument of restraint, it was the ultimate refuge of any group resisting the exercise of power. Jeffersonians invoked the Constitution against Hamilton; Federalists invoked it against Jefferson's Embargo and the purchase of Louisiana; Jackson used constitutional arguments in destroying the Bank of the United States; Whigs denounced Jackson for unconstitutionally exceeding his executive authority; Southern slaveholders relied increasingly upon the Constitution for protection of their "peculiar institution"; and seven words in the document enabled Dartmouth College to fight off state control. It was a rare public issue that did not involve constitutional debate, and the latter tended to replace the broader political theory of the Revolutionary era.

Such debate cannot be dismissed as empty rhetoric. Constitutional theory, even though it usually served to rationalize material interests, sometimes had a decisive effect upon public controversy. For example, the Constitution was plainly a barrier to any direct attack upon slavery in the states. The Western territories accordingly became the focus of sectional conflict, and the moral issue of slavery was inextricably tangled with the process of westward expansion. In short, constitutional abstractions were capable of giving direction and configuration to more elemental historical forces.

Of those forces, none was more pervasive than the cluster of attitudes and behavior patterns associated with the word "democracy." The democratic trend in politics was but one manifestation of the vigorous egalitarianism that characterized much of American life. Visitors from Europe were struck by the easy relations between persons of different social rank, even between masters and servants. An English matron in Cincinnati was utterly bewildered when her hired girl burst into tears at the announcement that she must eat in the kitchen. No English servant would have expected to dine with the family. But what the Englishwoman failed to understand was that the American girl did not think of herself as belonging to a permanent servant class. Indeed, before long she too might be the mistress of her own home, with her own hired "help." It was not the absence but the fluidity of class distinctions that made the difference. The high degree of social mobility encouraged expectations that bred an assumption of equality. One man was as good as another because of what he could become.

The democratic spirit permeated the whole fabric of American society. It was especially apparent in the demands for a more generous public land policy, in the growing opposition to economic privilege, and in the progress of evangelical Protestantism. Most significant of all, perhaps, were the beginnings of a public school system. In a democracy, free education plainly served both the need for an intelligent electorate and the principle of equal opportunity.

The idea of unlimited opportunity for individuals blended readily with belief in the perfectibility of human society, and great expectations led to dissatisfaction with existing conditions. By the 1830s, a variety of reform movements were under way, all testifying to the vitality of the democratic faith. Social change during this period resulted largely from the random play of many forces and purposes, but it was sometimes achieved by planned effort.

It is change that catches the historian's eye, while continuity often goes unnoticed. The result can be serious distortion of a past era by too much stress upon its cataclysmic features. Many striking changes did occur in America during the first half of the nineteenth century, but they are not the whole story. Tradition too was a powerful force, and the persistence of familiar customs, institutions, and values made national life a complex mixture of old ways and new.

When John Quincy Adams died, the United States was different, but not entirely different, from the nation that he had begun to serve more than fifty years earlier. Its people were still predominantly Anglo-Saxon in their language, customs, and laws. It was still a federal republic under a Constitution that had remained virtually unchanged, still primarily agricultural and decidedly Protestant. Emotional ties with the Revolutionary generation were as strong as ever, and indeed the Founding Fathers, growing in stature as they receded into the past, had become a pantheon of demigods. New England still honored Puritan virtues, and the cotton kingdom recapitulated the values of the colonial tidewater. If reverence for tradition is a conservative trait, then most Americans were in some degree devoted conservatives.

Furthermore, social change that occurs over a long period of time comes to be accepted as a normal condition of life and is thus a kind of continuity. Many of the changes experienced by Americans in the early nineteenth century were segments of arcs extending from the past into the future. Political democracy, for example, was not an exclusive achievement of the Jacksonian era. In some respects it had existed a hundred years earlier; in other respects it would still be incomplete a hundred years later. Westward expansion, with all its turbulence, was another continuous factor in American history.

The restless temper and the principal techniques of pioneering dated back to colonial times, and so did the Western land and Indian policies of the federal government. The phrase "manifest destiny" became popular in the 1840s, but the idea was older than the Republic. Behind the Southern defense of slavery lay the heritage of two centuries, and the first published attacks upon the institution had appeared long before the Revolution. The revivalism that became such a prominent feature of nineteenth-century religion was anticipated in the "great awakening" of the 1730s, and the emerging social reform movements of the Jacksonian period owed much to the old Puritan habit of self-examination.

One must also remember that large numbers of people were often affected only slightly or indirectly by a particular social change. Much of the South lagged far behind in the process of industrialization and urbanization. The Catholic Church stood relatively aloof from the religious ferment of the period. The westward movement, spectacular though it was, involved but a fraction of the population; at mid-century, for example, seven out of eight native New Englanders still lived in New England. And the phrase "Jacksonian democracy" has little meaning in American Negro history; for it was during this allegedly egalitarian era that Southern theorists elaborated their defense of slavery as a benign and natural institution, good for all time, while free Negroes in both the North and the South were being weighted down with increasing disabilities.

In addition, the forces of social change usually met sturdy resistance at every turn. Much of this resistance was relatively inarticulate and even unconscious—stemming from the natural tendency of a predominantly rural society to prefer the old, familiar ways and to view innovations with suspicion, apprehension, or indifference. One of the most striking examples was the persistence of smallpox. Inoculation had been introduced early in the eighteenth century, and before its close Edward Jenner discovered the miracle of vaccine. Thomas Jefferson, after vaccinating his own family and neighbors, wrote to Jenner: "You have erased from the calendar of human afflictions one of its greatest." Yet as late as the year 1920 there were over a hundred thousand cases of smallpox in the United States. There was also a good deal of articulate and organized hostility to change. Conservatives bitterly resisted the trend toward universal suffrage. Humanitarians denounced the removal of the Indians. Hard-money men fought a losing battle against paper currency. New England Whigs opposed the aggressive expansionism of the 1840s, just as New England Federalists had opposed the acquisition of Louisiana. Even when they failed, such elements often influenced the course of history.

Finally, a deep-set ambivalence frequently appeared in the thinking of individual Americans about their country and the changes that were overtaking it. Their exuberant national pride was honeycombed with feelings of cultural inferiority. They were torn between the desire to repudiate Europe and a hunger for Europe's praise. They celebrated the material progress of the nation, but mourned the passing of old virtues. Approval mixed with doubt in their reflections upon trends such as the growth of the factory system, the influx of immigrants, and the democratization of politics. They saw too much new ugliness to be convinced that change was synonymous with improvement. In James Fenimore Cooper and certain other writers of the period one sees the strain imposed by their perception of how much America was gaining and losing in the process of social change; and through many of the nineteenth-century reform movements, with all their emphasis on progress, ran a thread of nostalgia for better days past.

The fullest catalog of social changes is therefore never a complete record of the past. Yet change has nearly always been the dominant theme in historical writing because it lends itself to narrative moving through time, it poses the most exciting problems in causal analysis, and it draws the past toward the present. Except as pure entertainment, the study of history repays us primarily by revealing how we changed from what we were to what we are. In many ways, the first half of the nineteenth century in America may best be understood as an age of beginnings rather than climaxes. It was the seedtime of the industrial revolution, the prelude to sectional conflict, an early stage in the development of a democratic society. These generations saw the introduction of power-driven transportation, the rise of social reform, the start of mass immigration. The most climactic change of the period was the sweep of American sovereignty and American pioneers across the continent to the Pacific. That is why it may appropriately be labeled "The Era of Expansion."

Chapter II

The Jeffersonian Republic

A CHANGE OF LEADERSHIP

In 1800, the United States entered its twenty-fifth year of independence. The destinies of the Republic were nevertheless still entangled with those of Europe, where Napoleon Bonaparte, now the complete master of France, was smashing a Second Coalition of opposing powers. American pride and American maritime trade had suffered repeated blows during the Anglo-French struggle that dated from 1793. A dangerous quarrel with Great Britain subsided after the ratification of Jay's Treaty, but then American relations with France became inflamed. Disclosure of the "XYZ Affair" was followed by open hostilities between the two nations upon the high seas, and popular feeling in the United States was pushing the government toward a formal declaration of war. At this point, President John Adams deflated the martial spirit by resuming negotiations with France. The result was the Convention of 1800, an agreement that settled various matters in dispute and released the United States from its obligations under the Treaty of 1778.

Americans were sharply divided in their views of the French Revolution and of the convulsive European struggle that followed it. This division coincided generally with the intense disagreement over domestic policies that arose during Washington's first administration. Hamiltonian advocates of a strong central government and vigorous economic measures tended also to support England as the defender of social order against revolutionary anarchy. The Jeffersonian opposition, jealous of liberty and favoring the dispersal of power, embraced the French cause with an enthusiasm that declined but did not disappear when France became harder to admire. Gradually, the partisanship of the 1790s crystallized. The two opposing

An anti-Jefferson cartoon. He is detected by Providence in the act of sacrificing the Constitution on the altar of French despotism.

groups achieved identity, rudimentary organization, and a semblance of permanence. Contrary to all intentions of the founding fathers, the American party system had been born.

In the election of 1796, the contest between Federalists and Republicans was somewhat muted by Jefferson's willingness to settle for the vice-presidency and leave the higher office to his old friend, John Adams. But animosities aroused by the Alien and Sedition Acts set the stage for a fiercer confrontation in 1800. Meanwhile, Adams' decision to seek an understanding with France had frustrated Hamilton's ardent desire for war, and a bitter factional struggle within the ranks of Federalism was hastening its downfall.

It is easy to overstate the differences between the two new political parties and to overlook the underlying consensus that bound Americans together as a nation. Yet by 1800 certain tendencies were plain. The Federalists generally had a more patrician view of politics, a greater interest in mercantile enterprise, and a broader conception of the role to be played by government, especially the federal government, in national development. The Republicans professed greater faith in the ability of the people to rule themselves, insisted that the protection of liberty required strict limitations upon governmental power, and visualized an agricultural republic of freeholders. Although the Federalist outlook, in some respects, offered a clearer vision of the future, the Republicans were more in accord with the contemporary spirit of the nation. Jeffersonian ideals marched westward along the expanding agricultural frontier, while Federalism steadily retreated into its New England stronghold.

The presidential election of 1800 was therefore a sectional as well as a political contest. The Republicans, dominant in the South and the new West, also captured the pivotal state of New York, where Jefferson had long since found an ally and running mate in the person of Aaron Burr. At the same time, the Adams and Hamilton wings of the Federalist party were expending much of their energy in attacks upon each other. Despite all of these advantages, the Republicans did not sweep into power with a decisive victory. The election was close. Jefferson received 73 electoral votes to Adams' 65. Furthermore, to Jefferson's embarrassment, the Republican electors had likewise cast 73 ballots for Burr, and since the Constitution provided for no distinction between first and second places on a party ticket, the two men were tied for the presidency. This meant that the election was transferred to the House of Representatives. There a deadlock developed because many Federalists cynically chose to support the erratic and intensely ambitious New Yorker. Not until 36 ballots were taken did Jefferson receive a majority and become officially the President-elect.

Thus the Federalist era ended, and a generation of Republican leadership began. Yet the nation was still in the hands of its founders—men of the Revolution and the Age of Reason, who studied the theory while practicing the art of politics. Continuity with the past modulated the abrupt transfer of power. The Federalist structure of government and many Federalist policies were retained with but minor alterations. It was the temper and style of government that changed the most, thus becoming simpler, more democratic,

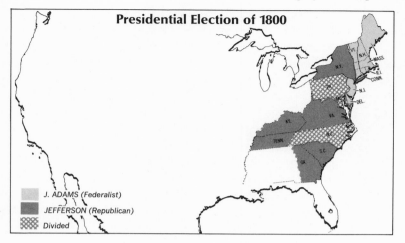

Presidential Election of 1800

J. ADAMS (Federalist)
JEFFERSON (Republican)
Divided

and less derivative. The inauguration of Jefferson accelerated the process of Americanization.

Many hands had built the Republican party, and Jefferson shared the role of chief architect with his friend James Madison. As scholar, pamphleteer, and legislative captain, Madison had made the more versatile contribution. But Jefferson, the apostle of American liberty in 1776 and the counterforce to Hamilton in the 1790s, was the very symbol of Republicanism and its natural leader. He set indelibly upon the party the imprint of his mind and personality. The history of Jefferson's administration clearly reflects his conviction that the main responsibilities of the federal government lay in the realm of foreign relations. Internal affairs, he believed, were primarily the concern of the states. The West, of course, was a special case, requiring extensive federal activity until new states could be created there. Otherwise the Jefferson domestic program was negative in tone. It stressed retrenchment, administrative efficiency, and the erasure of some Federalist handiwork like the excise tax and the Alien and Sedition Acts.

Standing aloof from Jeffersonian ascendancy in the executive and legislative branches was the federal judiciary. There the Republicans saw their enemies entrenched. An act of Congress, passed shortly before Jefferson's inauguration, had created many new judgeships. It was a needed reform, but Adams promptly filled all of these positions with Federalists. More important in the long run, he also installed John Marshall as Chief Justice. The Republicans regarded these maneuvers as a plot to thwart the will of the people. They struck back by repealing the Judiciary Act of 1801 and thus eliminating the newly created offices. They also attempted, with small success, to turn the impeachment power of Congress against the courts. Gradually, as the years passed, vacancies were filled by Jeffersonians, and yet the Supreme Court, under the firm direction of its Chief Justice, remained for decades a stronghold of Federalism.

Marshall, like Hamilton, was a conservative and a nationalist. In his hands, the Court became a guardian of property rights and of national supremacy— both at the expense of state sovereignty. The first important Marshall decision, *Marbury v. Madison* (1803), was consequently not a representative one, since it amounted to a strict interpretation of federal authority. Written with the partisan purpose of rebuking the Jefferson administration for refusing to deliver the commission of an Adams appointee, Marshall's opinion also asserted the power of the Supreme Court to declare an act of Congress unconstitutional and void. Although Marshall never again invoked the doctrine of judicial review in this manner, he had set an important precedent. The Marbury case is most significant, however, as early evidence of Marshall's determination to make the judiciary an independent and powerful force in American history.

THE PROFITS AND PROBLEMS OF NEUTRALITY

Jefferson entered the White House committed to a policy of peace, disentanglement from Europe, and reduction of the military establishment. Yet he was also resolved to protect the national interest, and his appointment of Madison as Secretary of State underlined the importance of foreign relations. Isolationist sentiment did not fit the realities of American trade with Europe and European empire in America. Tensions produced by the controversy over neutral rights at sea were somewhat relaxed in 1801. The quarrel with France had been settled, and the war in Europe was drifting toward the truce of Amiens. It was in this favorable setting that Jefferson ventured naval chastisement of the Barbary states, which for many years had exacted tribute from nations trading in the Mediterranean. But now danger threatened the Republic from another direction, as the ominous figure of Napoleon loomed up on its western border.

The great expanse of Louisiana, a Spanish colony since 1762, was ceded back to France in 1800. News of the transfer, which did not become a finality until two years later, caused such alarm in the United States that Jefferson even began to talk of forming an alliance with Great Britain. The main concern was over the mouth of the Mississippi River, natural outlet for the growing commerce of the Trans-Appalachian West. Free navigation and transshipment privileges at New Orleans had been wrung from a reluctant Spain in the Pinckney Treaty of 1795. Now the whole battle would presumably have to be refought with a new and mightier adversary. It was clearly a time for action, and early in 1803 Jefferson sent James Monroe to Paris as a special envoy. Together with the American minister, Robert R. Livingston, Monroe was instructed to negotiate for the purchase of New Orleans and Florida too, if it had been included in the Louisiana transfer.

Meanwhile, French military disasters in Santo Domingo had ruined Napoleon's plan for a New World empire, and in addition, he was about to resume hostilities with England. Louisiana, in these circumstances, became a liability, and so he decided to dispose of it for needed cash. Soon two surprised American diplomats found themselves pledging their government to pay $15 million for the whole vast region between the Mississippi and the Rocky Mountains. By one stroke of good fortune, the size of the United States had been doubled.

Jefferson had long been keenly interested in the Trans-Mississippi West, and he actually commissioned the famous Lewis and Clark expedition before Napoleon offered to sell Louisiana. The good news from Paris nevertheless caused the President some embarrassment, for the acquisition of territory was not expressly authorized by the Constitution. Having repeatedly denounced the doctrine of implied power, he now faced the necessity of invoking it. A constitutional amendment would consume too much time, and Napoleon might change his mind any day. So Jefferson laid aside his scruples and recommended ratification of the treaty. Approved by a special session of Congress, the Louisiana Purchase was the outstanding achievement of Jefferson's presidential career. It helped him to win reelection in 1804 with an overwhelming majority of the electoral vote.

By then, Americans were again reaping inflated profits as neutral traders in wartime. But as the renewed struggle between England and France grew more desperate, both nations adopted sterner measures to cut enemy supply lines. British orders and Napoleonic decrees restricting neutral shipping became so severe in 1806–1807 that Yankee captains could not obey one belligerent without defying the other. Enforcement by visit and search, with many seizures resulting, was incomplete but often high-handed. Superior

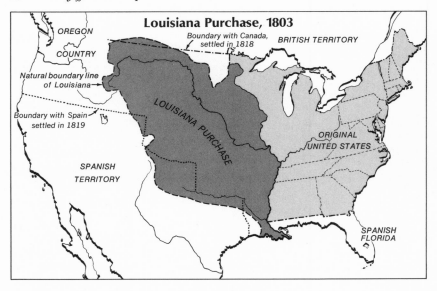

naval power made Britain the greater offender, and British impressment of sailors on American vessels caused repeated outbursts of anger in the United States. A crisis arose in June 1807, when the British *Leopard,* looking for deserters, attacked an American warship, the *Chesapeake,* killing three men and wounding many more. From an outraged public came passionate demands for full retaliation.

Jefferson, however, was resolved to maintain peace while defending American rights. Economic coercion of Europe, he believed, would serve both purposes. At his urging in December 1807, Congress passed the Embargo Act, which prohibited virtually all commerce with foreign countries. Here, truly, was an ambitious effort to contrive an effective substitute for war. Yet if the Embargo reflected Jefferson's idealism, it also violated his cherished principle of strict construction, and it disregarded his own solemn warnings against federal tyranny. Intended to punish Britain and France, the law, in fact, crippled the American economy and aroused fierce opposition, especially in New England. Widespread evasion provoked arbitrary methods of enforcement too much like those of British colonial officials before the Revolution. After fourteen troublous months, a frustrated Jefferson gave up the experiment. Just before leaving the presidency in March 1809, he signed legislation repealing the Embargo Act and substituting a

Non-Intercourse Act, which applied only to England and France. Since it permitted American ships to sail for other countries, this new version of peaceful coercion proved even harder to enforce.

Although Jefferson's second administration ended on a note of failure, he was able to secure the nomination of Madison as his successor by the party caucus in Congress. Factional and doctrinal quarrels were undermining Republican unity, however. A dissident group led by John Randolph in Virginia, deploring the drift away from old Jeffersonian principles, had tried unsuccessfully to promote James Monroe as a candidate. New York Republicans supported Vice-President George Clinton, and six presidential electors actually voted for him instead of Madison. From this time forward, the party of Jefferson would become increasingly a loose combination of sectional and personal factions.

Discord among their opponents and the growing unpopularity of the Embargo spelled opportunity for the Federalists, but they were unequal to it. Failure was becoming a habit with them. Even before the death of Hamilton at Burr's hands in 1804, Federalism suffered from a lack of constructive leadership. Born to power rather than achieving it, the party was slow to learn the techniques of organizational discipline and mass appeal. In defeat it became sour, parochial, and prone to sterile obstructionism. Fear of Western growth, for example, led Federalists to oppose the full incorporation of Louisiana into the Union. Falling back on constitutional arguments, they now embraced the old Jeffersonian doctrines of strict construction and states rights. Certain extremists like Timothy Pickering of Massachusetts went further and talked openly of secession. Thus Federalism, already stamped as the foe of democracy and expansion, was also tainted with disunionism. It regained control of New England in 1808, but Madison carried the rest of the country and replaced Jefferson in the White House.

THE WAR OF 1812

The new President had virtually inherited his office and with it the problem of extracting concessions from the European belligerents before their harassment of neutral shipping drove the American people to war. As chief executive in a time of sustained crisis, however, Madison was somewhat miscast. He did not have enough personal force to control his party or to give the nation a sense of direction. Alternately ingenuous and shrewd, impulsive and hesitant, he left the public confused about his purposes and seemed more feckless than he really was.

Efforts at economic coercion continued. The ineffective Non-Intercourse Act was replaced in 1810 by Macon's Bill No. 2, which invited Britain and France to compete for America's favor. The measure authorized resumption of commerce with both nations, but provided that if either belligerent withdrew its offensive maritime restrictions, the ships and goods of the other would be excluded from United States ports. Napoleon responded with a hollow pledge of repeal, and Madison hastily accepted it; when no equivalent gesture came from London, nonimportation was invoked against Britain. From this point on, Anglo-American relations deteriorated rapidly. The war spirit in the United States was intensified by an Indian uprising on the northwestern frontier, allegedly incited by British officials. In addition, a new group of militant young congressmen stiffened the will of the administration. An embargo enacted in April 1812 was both a preparation for hostilities and a last warning to England. Then, at Madison's request, a declaration of war followed in June. It met strong resistance, passing by votes of 79 to 49 in the House of Representatives and 19 to 13 in the Senate. Americans learned too late that the British government had already revoked its oppressive regulations shortly before the war began.

Thus, with a little luck, the nation could have avoided one of its most unpopular and least successful wars. Yet this does not mean that the decision in 1812 was made precipitately or for inconsiderable reasons. On the contrary, it climaxed nearly two decades of humiliation and recurring crises. For a majority of Americans, the price of peace had become too high, and the War of 1812 was in no small degree just what it purported to be—a defense of national honor. There were other influences, however, some reinforcing and some contravening the appeal to arms.

Opposition to the declaration of war reflected a certain amount of Federalist partisanship, pro-British feeling, and genuine pacifism. It was especially strong in the commercial centers of the Northeast because hostilities would no doubt mean blockade by the English fleet and ruin for the very mercantile interests that were ostensibly being defended. To Yankee ship-owners still recovering from the Embargo, the remedy again seemed far worse than the affliction. On the other hand, the move toward war received overwhelming support from Southern and Western states, where a persistent agricultural depression was blamed upon British interference with exports to Europe. Westerners also attributed their Indian troubles to the scheming of Canadian officials. Furthermore, the very existence of Canada encouraged American aggressiveness, for it made war with England feasible, offering a ready target for offensive action. The on-to-Canada enthusiasm was, at the same time, an expression of the expansionist spirit which had already led Madison to claim and occupy part of West Florida in 1810. Altogether, it seems abundantly clear that anger and pride, intense nationalism, and material interest were all involved in the decision to strike a second blow for independence.

Much as they favored war, the American people were wretchedly prepared for it, and not many of them wanted to do the actual fighting. The army was small and poorly commanded. Enlistments did not meet expectations. Government bonds sold too slowly. State militia sometimes refused to cooperate with federal forces, and maritime New England remained aloof, almost neutral in the contest. The assault on Canada turned into a series of fiascos, so that by the end of 1812, American troops were on the defensive all along the northern frontier. At sea, the small United States navy won some brilliant individual combats, but the tightening British blockade soon bottled it up. Only England's preoccupation with the struggle in Europe gave the Americans time to brace themselves against threatened disaster.

The situation began to improve in the latter part of 1813. Captain Oliver Hazard Perry's naval victory on Lake Erie enabled General William Henry Harrison to launch a counteroffensive which restored American power in the Northwest and neutralized some hostile Indian tribes of that region. Meanwhile, a part of the Creek nation in the Southwest was taking to the warpath, but General Andrew Jackson led his Tennessee militia against the Indians and crushed their resistance in the spring of 1814. American forces had already occupied Mobile and thus completed seizure of West Florida, claimed by Jefferson and Madison as part of the Louisiana Purchase. On the critical New York battlefront there were no equivalent gains. A renewed effort to attack Montreal ended in ignominious failure, and the conquest of Canada remained a vain hope.

The defeat and abdication of Napoleon in April 1814 released British energies for the war in North America. While a diversionary force was raiding and burning Washington, but failing to take Baltimore, about 10,000 troops marched southward from Canada along the familiar Lake Champlain route.

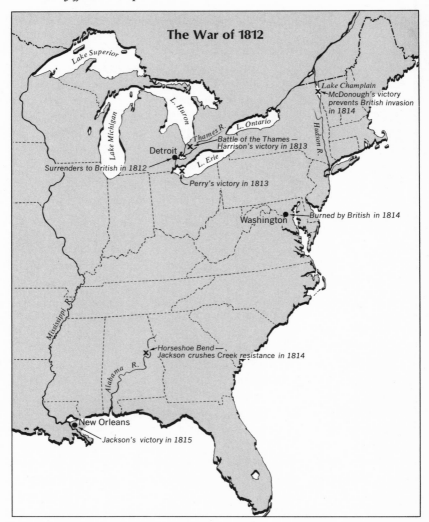

The War of 1812

Lake Superior

Lake Champlain
X—McDonough's victory
prevents British invasion
in 1814

L. Huron

Lake Michigan

L. Ontario

Thames R.

Battle of the Thames —
Harrison's victory in 1813

Detroit

Hudson R.

Surrenders to British in 1812

L. Erie

X
Perry's victory in 1813

Washington —Burned by British in 1814

Mississippi R.

Horseshoe Bend —
X—Jackson crushes Creek resistance in 1814

Alabama R.

New Orleans
Jackson's victory in 1815

Once again an inland naval engagement proved decisive. On September 11, the American fleet commanded by Thomas Macdonough won a complete victory over its British counterpart. Having lost control of the lake and meeting sturdier resistance on land, the invading forces withdrew. But then danger threatened from another quarter, as an imposing army of British veterans landed near New Orleans to strike at the Mississippi Valley. Jackson, now a United States major general, placed his motley troops in a strong defensive position before the city and, on January 8, 1815, administered a devastating defeat to the attacking regiments. For every American casualty there were a hundred on the British side—all of them cruelly unnecessary, since a treaty of peace had been signed two weeks before. The battle of New Orleans ended the fighting on a deceptive note of magnificent victory, and it also inaugurated the Jacksonian legend.

The first overtures for peace had been made in 1812, soon after the war started. They were unsuccessful largely because of American insistence upon the renunciation of impressment. A Russian offer of mediation also failed, but it led to an arrangement for direct negotiations, which began at Ghent in August 1814. John Quincy Adams, Henry Clay, and the other American commissioners found themselves on the defensive because the initiative in the war was obviously passing to Britain. The repulse of the invading army at Lake Champlain reduced the pressure, however. The British representatives eventually withdrew their territorial claims and other demands, while the Americans abandoned the fight against impressment. Signed on Christmas eve, the Treaty of Ghent did little more than restore the *status quo ante bellum.* Yet, in the United States, it was joyfully received; for if the war had gained nothing, Americans at this point were pleased to have lost nothing. Besides, with Europe returning to peace, maritime rights would no longer be a critical issue and impressment would presumably cease. As for American pride, it had been vindicated by the glamorous victory at New Orleans.

On December 15, 1814, as the negotiations at Ghent were nearing their conclusion, another meeting began at Hartford, Connecticut. Delegates from the five New England states assembled to vent the grievances of their section and to propose changes in the federal system. The convention was dominated by moderate Federalists rather than the extremists who had been demanding a separate peace with England. It approved resolutions in the states' rights tradition and proposed constitutional amendments aimed at restricting the political power of the South and West. New England, however, had withheld support of the war, had traded with the enemy, and had enjoyed favorable treatment from British blockade squadrons as a consequence. Against this background, the Hartford Convention appeared more subversive than it really was. Suffering ridicule because of its bad timing, it also became a symbol of treasonable conspiracy and added another stain to the already dubious reputation of Federalism.

THE NATION REORIENTED

Indecisive though the War of 1812 had been, its conclusion introduced a new period of American history. The Treaty of Ghent, coinciding with the end of the long conflict in Europe, signaled the release of powerful internal forces from the restraints previously imposed by external dangers. In addition, the mood of the country was being set more and more by a generation born since the Declaration of Independence and less responsive to European influences. "Nationalism," the word commonly used to characterize the postwar years, is accurate within limits and appropriate in more than one sense.

After 1815, the attention of the American people turned inward to domestic matters and the work of occupying a continent. Disentanglement from the political fortunes of the Old World had been an unattainable objective during the preceding decades, but now there began a century of comparative isolation and security for the United States, paralleled by a century of comparative peace in Europe. Against threats from abroad, the nation was protected by the same Atlantic Ocean that had been the scene of so much conflict. At the same time, dangers nearer home were progressively reduced by the elimination or neutralization of European power in the Western Hemisphere. The critical factor in both cases was the benevolent influence, only partly intended, of British strength and British foreign policy.

The Treaty of Ghent left Britain and the United States facing each other across a long border, but with increased mutual respect and a pronounced willingness to settle disputes by negotiation. Canada was still British and still vulnerable to American attack—a virtual hostage to peace that offset the supremacy of the Royal Navy in times of stress. The Rush-Bagot agreement of 1817, limiting the number of armed vessels on the Great Lakes, proved to be the first step in the establishment of an "unguarded frontier." A convention signed the following year redrew the northwestern boundary along the 49th parallel from the Lake of the Woods to the Rocky Mountains and provided for joint occupation of the Oregon country beyond. Disagreements and occasional crises continued to disturb Anglo-American relations throughout the century, but the disposition to negotiate instead of fight became a fixed habit.

To the south, meanwhile, the vast Spanish empire was falling apart. During the years 1810 to 1813, while Spain struggled in the grasp of Napoleon and revolution spread through Latin America, the United States had seized

West Florida. Spanish control of East Florida was also precarious, and American acquisition seemed to be only a matter of time. Indian troubles along the border led to an invasion of the colony in 1818 by federal troops under Andrew Jackson. This aggressive action helped to convince officials in Madrid that they could no longer resist American demands. In the Adams-Onis Treaty of 1819, Spain surrendered Florida, together with her claims to the Pacific Northwest. The United States, in return, agreed to assume as much as $5 million of private American claims against the Spanish government, and it also renounced a dubious claim to Texas as part of the Louisiana Purchase. Spanish procrastination delayed ratification of the treaty until 1821. By that time, Mexico had won its fight for independence, and the flag of Spain no longer flew anywhere on the North American continent.

The belief that America's destiny was different from Europe's destiny dated back to colonial times, but in the setting of the postwar years it acquired added relevance and force. National confidence was resurgent, the national domain had been extended, and many parts of the New World were imitating the United States in throwing off European rule. The American government formally recognized the young Latin American republics in 1822. Then, one year later, President James Monroe gave classic expression to the concept of separate hemispheres.

The famous Monroe Doctrine originated as nothing more than several paragraphs in the President's annual message to Congress of December 2, 1823. Written in collaboration with Secretary of State John Quincy Adams, it dealt with two distinct problems. One was the threat of Russian expansion on the Northwest Coast. More important were the indications that Spain might receive help from certain other European powers in reconquering some of her lost colonies. The British government, desiring to keep the new Latin American markets open, offered to join the United States in a declaration opposing such intervention, but Adams argued successfully for an independent pronouncement. With Russia in mind, Monroe first asserted that the American continents were "henceforth not to be considered as subjects for future colonization by any European powers." Then, maintaining that the political systems of the Old and New Worlds were "essentially different" from each other, he warned that any attempt by European monarchies to subdue the Latin American republics would be regarded as "the manifestation of an unfriendly disposition toward the United States." At the same time, the American government would continue to refrain from interfering in the "internal concerns" of European nations.

These bold words amounted to a statement of unilateral policy without much effective force, and the immediate practical effects were relatively slight. Negotiations with Russia, already well advanced, soon produced a treaty fixing the southern boundary of Alaska at 54°40′. As for the Latin American republics, it was primarily the sea power of a hostile Britain that compelled Spain and her allies to abandon their vague schemes of reconquest. Not until many years later would the Monroe Doctrine be translated into action. Furthermore, despite its unselfish tone and hemispheric scope, the document was essentially a manifestation of ebullient nationalism. Here, something not said in Monroe's message is especially significant. Nowhere did he bind the United States itself to the principles of noncolonization and nonintervention in Latin America. The British government had included a self-denying provision in its general proposal for joint action, but American leaders, with their eyes on Cuba and Texas, were not to be caught in such a trap. Thus the Monroe Doctrine extended the horizons of American ambition and served as a preface to Manifest Destiny.

Nationalism in the form of disengagement from Europe can also be seen in postwar efforts to obtain a larger measure of economic self-sufficiency and in appeals for cultural independence. Yet the United States continued to be, in many respects, a colonial society, still heavily dependent upon the Old World for markets, manufactured goods, capital, people, ideas, and tastes. The reorientation that began in 1815 was more a shift of attention than a renunciation. Indeed, it may be regarded as the natural sequel of the Revolution, delayed for two decades by the abnormal condition of world affairs.

TRANSITIONAL YEARS

In its internal aspect, the nationalism of this period seemed to confirm Hamilton's design for the Republic. With patriotism vindicated at New Orleans and sectional feeling discredited at Hartford, the country was apparently ready to accept vigorous leadership from the federal government. Congress responded by enacting a protective tariff, establishing a new national bank, and proposing to subsidize construction of inland transportation facilities. Thus the Jeffersonians continued to appropriate the old Federalist program. Yet this change of attitude, which had begun before the war, fell far short of being a complete surrender to the Hamiltonian ideal of a consolidated state. The decade after 1815 was a time of contradictory tendencies and shifting allegiances in which nationalism as the equivalent of centralization actually made little headway.

The responsibilities of power had caused the Jeffersonians to set aside their worst fears of the central government and to compromise some of their old constitutional principles. They had even come eventually to a grudging acceptance of the Bank of the United States. Madison and his Secretary of the Treasury, Albert Gallatin, recommended renewal of the Bank's charter when it expired in 1811, but a combination of hostile groups in Congress defeated the necessary legislation. The lack of a fiscal agent severely handicapped the government during the War of 1812. Accordingly, Congress reversed itself in 1816 by establishing a second Bank of the United States, with authorized capitalization of $35 million and the government a one-fifth shareholder. Enemies of the institution were not silenced, however. The battle merely shifted to the state level, where the various branches of the Bank often met fierce opposition from local enterprise. As an expression of nationalism, the revival of the Bank was a very limited victory at best.

Expediency also governed the tariff legislation of 1816. Industries, stimulated by the long interruption of normal trade with Europe, suddenly faced ruinous competition from abroad after the war. In setting the rates on dutiable goods at 15 to 30 percent ad valorem, Congress was meeting an obvious need and making only a moderate concession to the principle of protection. The act consequently received support from all parts of the nation—even from many Southerners, like John C. Calhoun, who expected their section to share in the benefits. Circumstances soon produced dramatic changes, however. In spite of the tariff, imports from Europe continued to flood the United States, and the Panic of 1819 introduced a period of widespread economic distress. Western farmers and urban workers now joined the manufacturing interests in demanding higher duties to protect their respective products. Meanwhile, with the cotton kingdom expanding rapidly and depending more and more upon the foreign market, Southerners closed ranks in bitter hostility to protection. Thus feelings on both sides were sharply intensified, and the tariff became an explosive sectional issue in the 1820s.

More nationalistic in its implications than the Bank or the tariff was Calhoun's Bonus Bill of 1817, earmarking certain government funds for internal improvements. As a precedent, supporters of the measure could point to the Cumberland Road, authorized during Jefferson's administration and still under construction. Jefferson, in fact, had recommended an extensive system of federal roads and canals, but with the assumption that it would require an amendment to the Constitution. Calhoun's argument that such expenditures were permissible under the general welfare clause did not convince Madison, who vetoed the Bonus Bill, even though he approved of its purpose. His successor, Monroe, displayed the same constitutional scruples. Internal-improvements legislation also met persistent opposition from New England and the Old South, sections that had little to gain from rapid development of the West. A comprehensive federal program therefore never materialized, and the task of providing transportation facilities was left, for the most part, to the states and private enterprise.

It was the Supreme Court that gave the most emphatic expression to the spirit of nationalism during the postwar decade. John Marshall's decision in *McCulloch v. Maryland* (1819) upheld the constitutionality of the Bank of the United States and rescued it from excessive state taxation. More than that, in ringing phrases Marshall asserted the Hamiltonian doctrine of implied powers and broad construction of the Constitution. In *Cohens v. Virginia* (1821), the Court reaffirmed its authority to review decisions of state courts, and in *Gibbons v. Ogden* (1824), it laid down a broad definition of federal power under the commerce clause. The Dartmouth College decision (1819) extended the meaning of "contract" to include a corporate charter, thus interposing a clause of the Constitution as a protective screen between the authority of a state government and the private rights of its own citizens. The general effect of this judicial nationalism was to place immediate restraints upon the states and to lay the foundation for later expansion of federal power. The posture of the Court is commonly attributed to Marshall's success in imposing Federalist principles upon his Republican colleagues, but it also reflected the significant changes in Jeffersonian thinking that had occurred since 1800.

In politics after the War of 1812, there was a deceptive appearance of national consensus. With Madison's second term drawing to a close in 1816, the Republican congressional caucus nominated Secretary of State James Monroe for the presidency. Monroe won an easy victory in what proved to be the last stand, nationally, of the Federalist party. Four years later, he was reelected with just one dissenting vote in the electoral college. Republican ascendancy had become complete and therefore much less meaningful. The disappearance of organized Federalist opposition put an end, temporarily, to party politics and left faction as the only vehicle of partisanship. Underneath the semblance of unity in the so-called "era of good feelings," a process of fragmentation was erasing the Republican synthesis and introducing a political revolution.

Indeed, the almost unanimous presidential election of 1820 took place during the later stages of a violent controversy that had cut an angry and ominous gash across the nation. Early in 1819, when the application of Missouri for admission to statehood came before Congress, an antislavery amendment to the enabling act aligned Northerners against Southerners in a legislative struggle that lasted two years. Here was the very issue that would eventually disrupt the Union. It aroused Federalist hopes and revealed the thinness of the Republican consensus, but sectional loyalties were not yet strong enough to transform politics. This first great conflict over slavery ended in compromise. Congress admitted Missouri as a slave state and Maine (separated from Massachusetts) as a free state, thus preserving the sectional balance. More important for the future, slavery was forbidden north of 36°30' in the remainder of the Louisiana Purchase. These arrangements seemed to settle the dangerous issue completely and permanently. The sectional confrontation therefore ceased, and politics returned to familiar channels.

Monroe presided over a period of such change, complexity, and contradiction that it cannot be summed up with a label or descriptive phrase. The glow of postwar nationalism, for instance, was never universal, and it soon began to fade. Yet sectional rivalry did not dominate the scene,

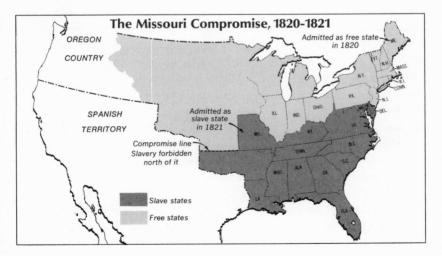

The Missouri Compromise, 1820-1821

OREGON COUNTRY

Admitted as free state in 1820

SPANISH TERRITORY

Admitted as slave state in 1821

Compromise line — Slavery forbidden north of it

Slave states

Free states

except in the Missouri episode. The interests of each section were shifting rapidly, and attitudes had only partly congealed. For political parties, too, it was a time of transition. The superficial harmony of Monroe's presidential tenure signified the inadequacy of old alignments and issues, not a decline of partisanship. This, the election of 1824 would clearly reveal. In a republic of free men, as the Jeffersonians had demonstrated, one party was not enough.

THE JEFFERSONIAN TRADITION

Monroe, the last Jeffersonian president, left the White House in 1825. Thus ended the "Virginia dynasty" which, for all but four years, had controlled the executive branch of the government. Jefferson died the next year on July 4, just a few hours before John Adams. It was the fiftieth anniversary of Independence, and to a nation growing in self-awareness, this solemn coincidence seemed like a miraculous seal upon the early history of the Republic. The Jeffersonian era had ended, but the Jeffersonian tradition grew in potency as the years went by. Each succeeding generation assimilated the image of Jefferson to its own experience and needs. All major political parties, and many of the minor ones, claimed descendance from him. In almost every significant discussion of public policy, he was summoned as an authority, usually on more than one side of the question.

It was more often Jefferson's ideas than his example that posterity cited, and this tended to make a doctrinaire out of a man whose philosophy had actually been the counterpart of continuing experience. Earlier Jeffersonian principles were not abandoned after 1800, but neither did they remain unchanged by the responsibilities of power. The agrarian view of society and the libertarian concept of government had to be modified in the face of insistent realities. Strict constitutionalism gave way to opportunity in the purchase of Louisiana, and the War of 1812 revealed that the doctrine of states' rights could become a danger instead of a refuge. This constant tugging between old ideals and new circumstances produced not only change but an accumulated variety in the fabric of Jeffersonian thought.

Furthermore, in its dual commitment to individual liberty and the sovereignty of the people, Jefferson's political credo embodied the fundamental dilemma of American democracy. The potential conflict between these two ideas was not obvious at the beginning of the nineteenth century.

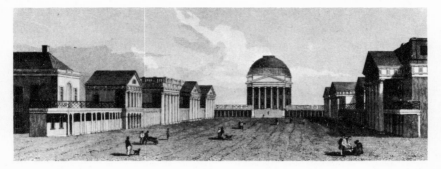

One of Jefferson's architectural achievements: the rotunda of the University of Virginia, 1831.

Both, after all, were major items of Republican armament in the battle against the aristocratic doctrines of Federalism. Besides, Jefferson conceived of popular sovereignty in localized, individualistic terms, rather than as a consolidated national will. But within a generation after his death, the Jeffersonian tradition had separated into two distinct and contrary strains of thought. One stressed freedom through restraint of power, or minority rights; the other stressed democratic use of power, or majority rule. Thus Jefferson could be invoked by both sides in the sectional controversy of the 1850s, and by both sides in the debates over "free enterprise" and the "welfare state" a century later. Inner contradiction and flexibility in practice made Jeffersonian liberalism a universal arsenal for subsequent political argument.

As a political leader, on the other hand, Jefferson has been somewhat less appreciated. His presidential reputation rests primarily upon the Louisiana windfall, and neither of his Republican successors is considered an outstanding chief executive. Yet it was the Jeffersonians who added the most important unofficial amendment to the American constitutional system by creating a party of opposition. The Federalist concept of government-by-consensus left no room for organized dissent. Only in a random way could the voice of the people be heard. The two-party system institutionalized controversy and provided the means for orderly transfer of power. Beginning with Jefferson's victory in 1800, certain presidential elections were to be the American equivalent of political revolutions.

Jefferson continued to be a party leader after entering the White House, despite his soothing inaugural words: "We are all Republicans; we are all

Federalists." This changed the nature of the presidential office from the Olympian magistracy of Washington. Wanting loyal subordinates in his administration, Jefferson made enough partisan dismissals and appointments to qualify as the originator of the "spoils system." Working through the majority leader and party caucus in Congress, he used his political power to direct the course of legislation. The result was a degree of operating unity in the federal government that partly offset the formal separation of powers. In joining the roles of party leader and legislative leader to the constitutional functions of his office, Jefferson completed the general framework of the modern presidency. Thus Jeffersonian practice, as well as Jeffersonian thought, shaped the American political tradition.

Chapter III

The Expanding Nation

THE FRONTIER PROCESS AND THE TRANS-APPALACHIAN WEST

The Jeffersonians were nowhere more persistent and unambiguous than in their zeal for national expansion. They added Louisiana and Florida to the national domain, tried to conquer Canada, and secured a half interest in the Pacific Northwest. Many of them believed that the acquisition of Cuba was only a matter of time; some were already turning covetous eyes upon the regions to the southwest; and the most exuberant spirits envisioned a nation extending from sea to sea and from the polar regions to Panama. Jefferson doubted that the Republic could grow much larger without becoming unmanageable, or worse, imperialistic in the European fashion. Instead, he contemplated the movement of American settlers to distant parts of the continent and the erection of new republics, bound to the United States only by "the ties of blood and interest." It was therefore the westward march of pioneers that would extend the area of freedom to its utmost limits.

Jefferson's confidence in the expansive force of the American population was inspired by what he saw happening during the era of Republican ascendancy. At the time of his first inauguration, about 10 percent of the people lived west of the Appalachians—most of them in Tennessee, Kentucky, and western Virginia. When Monroe left the presidency twenty-four years later, the proportion had risen to almost 30 percent. Settlement had crossed the Mississippi, and fur traders were ranging over wide areas of the Far West. Every year for six years, beginning in 1816, a new state entered the Union. The tempo and scale of national growth tended to intoxicate the imagination.

Behind the spectacular acceleration of westward migration in the nineteenth century lay many generations of pioneering experience. The first American West had been the back country of the seaboard colonies. There, the major characteristics and techniques of the frontier process had made their appearance: the lure of the virgin wilderness; exploration by hunters and traders; the ubiquity of land speculators; settlement by pioneer farmers; the arduous work of clearing trees, building cabins, breaking the soil, and planting crops; Indian raids and defense measures; the primitiveness and isolation of daily life; and the struggle to reproduce, in a new environment, the social order and physical comforts abandoned with the old home.

Expansion of the English colonial frontier was relatively slow because of the mountain barriers, the Indian menace, and the opposing power of France and Spain. In addition, the pressure of population increase did not become significant until the latter part of the eighteenth century. On the eve of the Revolution, large areas of upper New England, New York, and Pennsylvania were still unsettled, and at the southern end of the thirteen colonies, Georgia was little more than a foothold in the wilderness. Along the middle border, however, the westward movement had crossed the Appalachian range to the headwaters of the Ohio and Tennessee Rivers, while the boldest pioneers were pressing into the bluegrass region of Kentucky.

Even during the dangerous years of the Revolution, the westward advance of American settlers continued, and the peace treaty confirmed the new republic in possession of the vast area between the Appalachians and the Mississippi. Maryland, by refusing for more than three years to ratify the Articles of Confederation, had won general acceptance of the principle that the West belonged to the whole nation. Of the seven states claiming Western lands, six made cessions to the United States during the 1780s, while Georgia held out until 1802. Thus, at an early date, much of the Trans-Appalachian region became a responsibility of the central government, and the frontier problems that British officials had tried vainly to solve before 1776 were now laid before Congress. The most urgent task was pacification of the Indians at a time when eager settlers, speculators, and traders were invading their lands.

REMOVING THE INDIAN

The fate of the North American Indian was clearly written before the close of the eighteenth century. Frenchmen had accommodated their trading empire to his way of life, and there had always been a place for him in the Spanish colonial design. But the French were gone and Spanish power was waning. The Indian stood exposed to the aggressive energy and numerical preponderance of the Anglo-Americans, who generally regarded him as an obstacle to be removed like a stump in the roadway. Whether he chose resistance or submission made scarcely any difference in the end; for the diseases of the white man were even deadlier than his guns, and friendly tribes fared little better than hostile ones. Unable to halt the advance of American pioneers or to assimilate with their civilization, the Indian came sooner or later to his own bitter version of the westward movement.

The Indian problem, primarily a matter of military defense during the Revolution, became more complex when the war ended and the United States inherited the duties of the British Crown. The government's task, essentially, was to maintain peace on a rapidly moving frontier. This meant regulating trade with the Indians and especially traffic in weapons and liquor; opening up lands for settlement by negotiating treaties of cession with the appropriate tribes; and guarding the rights of the Indians as well as the safety of the white men. To some extent, therefore, the government played a mediating role in the everlasting conflict between Indians and settlers, although the settlers, of course, had first claim upon its sympathies and services.

In the dispossession of one race by another, however, violence could scarcely be avoided, and efforts to minimize it were hindered by various cultural and historical factors. The United States conducted its Indian diplomacy in terms that the Indian understood dimly at best. European concepts of territorial sovereignty, land tenure, and legal contract were alien to his experience, and the procedures of European statecraft did not suit his loosely organized, undisciplined social order. Treaties solemnly concluded with alleged tribal representatives (often in an atmosphere of duress or alcoholic persuasion) carried scant conviction among a highly individualistic people who had no written language and only rudimentary political institutions. On the other hand, the United States was chronically incapable of restraining its own citizens from lawless intrusions upon Indian land and other hostile acts. Both sides continually violated treaties and broke the peace.

Indian warfare, moreover, had long been a part of the European struggle for empire in North America, and this continued to be the case after the Revolution. Spanish officials used alliances with the Creeks and other tribes to impede American penetration of the Southwest, while the British kept possession of American forts in the Northwest and encouraged Indian resistance to settlement north of the Ohio. The expectation of help from the outside stiffened the Indian's determination and obscured the ultimate hopelessness of his cause. Indian relations were further complicated by the actions of state, territorial, and local governments on the frontier, since these agencies usually reflected the inflammatory impatience of the pioneer. The official policy of the United States was consequently only one of several influences shaping the course of events.

It required a dozen years of military action and negotiation after 1783 to establish a semblance of peace on the Indian frontier. To the south, a gifted Creek leader named Alexander McGillivray played off Spain against the United States in resisting the advance of Georgia settlers and speculators. But Spanish aggressiveness declined after 1790, and so did the Indian danger in the Southwest. Meanwhile, the Ohio country was the area of conflict in the north. With encouragement from nearby British officials, many tribes repudiated the treaties of cession extracted from them in 1784 to 1786. During the intermittent war that resulted, American forces first suffered two serious defeats, but at the battle of Fallen Timbers in 1794, an army commanded by General Anthony Wayne broke the Indian spirit of defiance. Wayne then dictated the Treaty of Greenville, which extinguished Indian land rights in the greater part of Ohio. This was soon followed by treaties with Great Britain and Spain securing the surrender of the Northwest posts and the disputed Yazoo strip in the Southwest. Thereafter, Indian troubles subsided for more than a decade.

The volume of westward migration after 1795 soon produced further demands for Indian land. When Jefferson became president, he did not let humanitarian scruples interfere with his ardent expansionism. New cessions were ruthlessly extorted from tribes in every section of the Trans-Appalachian frontier. William Henry Harrison, governor of Indiana Territory from 1800 to 1812, secured no less than fifteen such treaties during his tenure. The Indians of the Northwest, their anger steadily mounting, gravitated to the energetic leadership of two Shawnee brothers, Tecumseh and the Prophet, who organized an impressive tribal confederation to resist Harrison's policies. A border war was already beginning in 1811 when Tecumseh decided to visit the Southern tribes and enlist their aid. Taking advantage of his absence, Harrison led an army against the Indians concentrated on the upper Wabash. The ensuing battle of Tippecanoe was really not very decisive. It scattered the Indians and, to some extent, disrupted their confederation, but the attacks on outlying settlements continued.

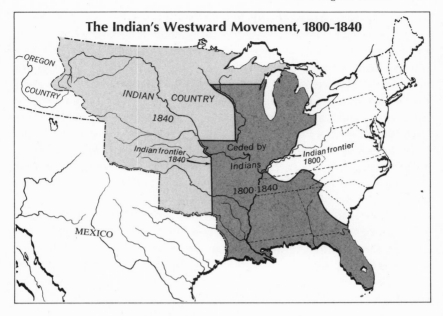

The Indian's Westward Movement, 1800-1840

OREGON COUNTRY

INDIAN COUNTRY 1840

Indian frontier 1840

Ceded by Indians

Indian frontier 1800

1800-1840

MEXICO

The Indian uprising merged into the War of 1812, as Tecumseh and many of his followers joined forces with the British. Among the Southern tribes, only a part of the Creek nation took up arms against the United States, and Jackson's victory at Horseshoe Bend eliminated the threat from that quarter. Along the far edge of the Old Northwest, however, the Indians retained the initiative until the end of the war. They were relying heavily upon the British promise to secure the erection of an Indian barrier state between the Ohio River and the Great Lakes. To their bitter disappointment, the Treaty of Ghent contained no such provision, although the British negotiators had made some efforts to obtain it. The War of 1812 was the last conflict in which the Indians could ally themselves with a European power to attack the American frontier. After that, they stood alone in their struggle for survival.

The efforts of the United States to protect and "civilize" the Indians were less successful than its military campaigns against them. Dishonest traders, whiskey peddlers, and trespassers upon Indian land could seldom be punished or even discouraged, while the natives themselves often seemed to learn only the vices of Anglo-American culture. Neither federal annuities nor the labor of resident agents and missionaries arrested a general trend toward impoverishment and degradation. Some tribes simply refused to give up their seminomadic ways, but those making substantial progress by the white man's standards were likewise regarded as a serious problem. Many of the Cherokees, for example, had settled down to agriculture and domestic industry on their remaining land, most of which was in Georgia. They developed a written language, published a newspaper, and organized their own "sovereign" republic under a written constitution. For Georgia, however, all of this was intolerable, especially since removal of the Indians had been promised when the state ceded its Western lands to the federal government in 1802. Whatever achievements they could claim, the Cherokees and all other tribes east of the Mississippi remained unassimilated elements in a hostile society. Even some of their staunchest friends concluded that the Indians should move to a new homeland beyond the Western frontier.

Relocation of the Indians was advocated by Jefferson at the time of the Louisiana Purchase, but it did not become a major public issue until after the War of 1812. Then, with settlers pouring into the Mississippi Valley, the proposal gained momentum. While a prolonged debate on the subject ran its course, federal officials began to implement the policy in specific cases. Consequently, a number of tribes had already been persuaded or compelled to migrate when Congress finally passed a general Removal Act in 1830. President Andrew Jackson, the frontiersman's friend, carried out the program with relentless vigor, and only the Seminoles in Florida fought a serious war of resistance. Nearly 100,000 Indians, suffering pitifully from exposure, sickness, and mistreatment, were herded westward along this "trail of tears." By 1840, the work was largely completed, and maps of the United States showed a "permanent" Indian frontier running along the western boundaries of Arkansas and Missouri, then across eastern Iowa and northern Wisconsin. Beyond that line the transplanted tribes struggled for survival against the elements and hostile neighbors, the Plains Indians. Soon they would also be afflicted by the renewed encroachments of the pioneer.

In the Eastern states, there was much condemnation of the removal policy, which went against the humanitarian grain of the 1830s. Yet no one could offer an alternative consistent with the realities of national life. Racial and cultural barriers excluded the Indian, while the westward movement irresistibly enveloped him, and thus he was always caught between the hammer of American energies and the anvil of American prejudice.

An artist's impression of Indian removal from their lands.

WESTERN LANDS

Virgin land was the magnet that drew Americans steadily westward. Before the Revolution, settlers acquired title to land from their respective colonial governments. But as a result of the various state cessions (1781–1802) and the Louisiana Purchase, most of the region between the Appalachians and the Rockies became public domain—that is, the property of the United States. The biggest exceptions were Kentucky, which Virginia did not cede, and Tennessee, already covered with private claims at the time of its cession by North Carolina. Federal ownership of Western land amounting to more than a million square miles was obviously temporary. No one doubted that much of the public domain would eventually be cleared of Indian occupancy and turned over to individual Americans. The purpose and means of federal land disposal were often at issue, however, and the policies adopted could not fail to have profound influence upon national development.

The first step in establishing a national land system was the Ordinance of 1785, which applied to the region northwest of the Ohio River. This measure reflected the conservative view that the public domain ought to yield a substantial revenue and that it should be sold in an orderly manner. Rejecting the looser practices of Virginia and other Southern states, Congress proposed to offer government land for sale only in rectangular parcels specifically designated by careful survey. The ordinance provided for the measuring off of townships six miles square, each divided into thirty-six numbered sections of one square mile or 640 acres. Half of the land would be sold in sections, half in entire townships. Sales were to be at auction, with $1 an acre as the minimum price.

The Ordinance of 1785 inaugurated a sound policy of orderly sales with clear titles, but it did not come to terms realistically with the needs of the frontiersman. A tract of 640 acres was too large for the average settler and too expensive, especially after 1796, when Congress raised the minimum price to $2 an acre. In addition, surveys lagged behind the advance line of settlement, and the status of innumerable "squatters," who occupied public domain without legal right, became a major political issue. Pressure from the West gradually produced changes in the land system which made it more favorable to actual settlers.

The Land Act of 1800 introduced a four-year credit system and allowed purchases of half sections (320 acres). In 1804, the minimum size was further reduced to 160 acres. These liberalized terms, together with the extension of surveys to the Southwest as a result of the Georgia cession in 1802, produced an increasing volume of land sales that reached one million acres annually by 1815. Yet the credit system proved unsatisfactory. The number of overdue payments mounted steadily, and pleas for more time became habitual. The Panic of 1819 finally brought matters to a crisis. In the Land Act of 1820, Congress reestablished the policy of selling public land only for cash, but it also lowered the minimum price to $1.25 an acre and fixed the minimum size of sales at 80 acres. Thus a settler could now buy a small farm directly from his government for as little as $100.

There remained the problem of the squatter, a trespasser upon the public domain, but also a popular symbol of the pioneering spirit. Did he have some measure of natural right to the land that he had illegally occupied and cultivated, or should it be sold at auction in the usual manner? For many years federal law incorporated the latter view, and yet squatters often managed to protect their interests by forming extralegal "claims associations" to discourage nonresidents from bidding up prices at public land sales. Eventually, Congress yielded to Western demands. In a series of acts passed between 1830 and 1841, it installed the principle of pre-emption, allowing actual settlers to buy as much as 160 acres at the minimum price of $1.25 an acre. Not satisfied with this victory, spokesmen for the pioneer began to argue that he should be given land free of charge, and during the next two decades, the homestead movement became the new center of attention.

Pre-emption was regarded then and later as a triumph of stalwart pioneers over greedy speculators, but these two interest groups were not mutually exclusive or invariably antagonistic. Everyone involved in the westward movement understood the opportunities offered by rising land values, and residents no less than absentee investors were usually ready to sell out at the right price. The speculative outlook was a universal characteristic of the frontier. Although the rapacity of speculators has not been exaggerated, many of them played useful roles as middlemen, selling land to settlers on easier terms and in smaller quantities than they could obtain from the government. Town-site speculation yielded the biggest profits, and as a consequence, sensitivity to land values colored local frontier politics. The location of a road, a bridge, a post office, or a county seat could make some men rich and others resentful.

Survey of the Public Domain

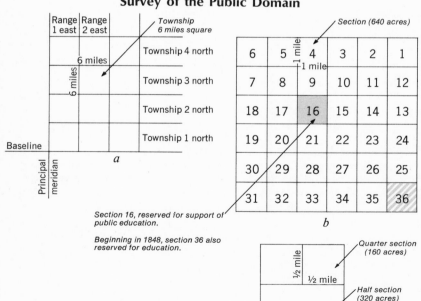

BY THE PRESIDENT OF THE UNITED STATES.

IN pursuance of an act of Congress, approved on the eleventh day of July, 1846, entitled " An act to authorize the President of the United States to sell the reserved mineral lands in the States of Illinois and Arkansas, and Territories of Wisconsin and Iowa, supposed to contain lead ore," I, JAMES K. POLK, PRESIDENT OF THE UNITED STATES OF AMERICA, do hereby declare and make known, that public sales of the lands HERETOFORE WITHHELD FROM SALE, in the State of ILLINOIS, ON ACCOUNT OF THE VALUABLE LEAD MINES THEREIN, will be held at the undermentioned Land Offices, in said State, at the periods hereinafter designated, to wit :

At the Land Office at DIXON, commencing on Monday, the fifth day of April next, for the disposal of the public lands within the following townships and fractional townships, viz :

North of the base line and east of the fourth principal meridian.

Fractional townships twenty-seven, twenty-eight, and twenty-nine, of range one.
Townships twenty-seven and twenty-eight, and fractional township twenty-nine, of range two.
Townships twenty-seven and twenty-eight, and fractional township twenty-nine, of range three.
The north half of township twenty-seven, township twenty-eight, and fractional township twenty-nine, of range four.

North of the base line and west of the fourth principal meridian.

Fractional townships twenty-seven, twenty-eight and twenty-nine, of range one.
Fractional townships twenty-eight and twenty-nine, of range two.

At the Land Office at SHAWNEETOWN, commencing on Monday, the nineteenth day of April next, for the disposal of the public lands within the following sections, and parts of sections, viz :

South of the base line and east of the third principal meridian.

Sections *twenty-two* to *twenty-nine*, inclusive, and sections *thirty-two* to *thirty-six*, inclusive, of township eleven ; sections *one* to *five* inclusive, and sections *eight* to *twelve*, inclusive, in township twelve, of range seven.
Sections *three* to *nine*, inclusive, sections *fifteen* to *twenty-two*, inclusive, and sections *twenty-five* to *thirty-six*, inclusive, of township eleven ; sections *one, two, three*, the north half and southeast quarter of section *four;* sections *five* to *eleven*, inclusive ; the southwest quarter of section *twelve;* the north half of section *fourteen*, and sections *fifteen* to *eighteen*, inclusive, in township twelve, of range nine.

Poster announcing sale of Federal land in Illinois, 1846.

The public land question was also a pervasive factor in national politics, and it tended to sharpen the differences between the West and other sections of the country. Easterners feared that a prodigal land policy would drain away the population and undermine the economy of the seaboard states. They insisted, moreover, that the public domain was a national treasure, to be used for the benefit of all the American people. The Eastern attitude found expression in Henry Clay's Distribution Bill, joined to the Pre-emption Act of 1841, but effective for only a brief period. Under this measure, most of the proceeds from land sales were to be divided among the various states according to their representation in Congress. Southerners, on the other hand, were afraid that any substantial reduction of federal revenue from public lands would furnish an excuse for raising tariff rates. Later, they also opposed the homestead movement because it seemed inimical to the expansion of slavery. Yet as the West grew in political power with the addition of new states, its desires carried ever-increasing weight.

The Pre-emption Act of 1841 marked the demise of the old conservative land policy with its emphasis upon revenue. Thereafter, despite strong opposition from some quarters, the trend was toward greater liberality, culminating in the Homestead Act of 1862. The government, furthermore, did not restrict its generosity to individual settlers. Since 1785, one section in each township had been set aside for the support of public schools; in 1848 this standard grant was doubled. Beginning in 1824, the states of the Old Northwest received gifts of several million acres to help finance the construction of canals, but they were dwarfed by the land grants for railroads in the 1850s and after. In these ways and various others, the public domain was lavishly committed to the rapid development of the country.

The abundance of virgin land undoubtedly reinforced democratic tendencies in American society. Nothing had contributed more to the exclusion of feudalism from the English colonies. In the frontier environment, traditional standards for judging a man's worth were radically modified. The swift opening of the West in the early nineteenth century offered opportunities not only to pioneer farmers but to adventurous businessmen, professionals, and politicians who headed for the new towns springing up on the advancing lines of settlement. Physical mobility promoted social mobility in a continually recurring equalitarian setting. Yet if Western land had a leveling effect, it could also be exploited in ways that increased economic inequality and produced crude aristocracies of wealth even on the rawest frontiers. Indeed, the influences of natural abundance upon American culture were so diverse and pervasive that they cannot be reduced to a simple formula.

WESTERN TERRITORIES AND THE GROWTH OF THE REPUBLIC

Besides the problems of Indian relations and land disposal, Congress also had to provide a system of government for the region west of the Appalachians. Nothing approximating colonialism was acceptable to a people who had just freed themselves from colonial status. The various state cessions were made with the clear understanding that the West would eventually become a group of new and equal states in an enlarged Union. But some arrangement must be made for the period of transition from wilderness to commonwealth. The West needed a form of government suitable for a population growing up to statehood.

After several years of discussion, the Congress functioning under the Articles of Confederation responded with the historic Northwest Ordinance of 1787. This measure authorized the ultimate formation of three to five states from the region north of the Ohio River, and it provided a state-making process in three stages. At first, the territory would be governed autocratically by appointed officials. As soon as the free adult males numbered 5000, it was to have a bicameral legislature and a nonvoting delegate in Congress. When the population as a whole reached 60,000, the territory could draft a constitution and apply for admission as a state.

Although details were changed, the Northwest Ordinance remained the model for all subsequent territorial organization. In many respects, it reproduced the conservative form of government existing in the royal colonies before the Revolution. The governor and upper house of the assembly were appointed—by Congress at first, by the President after the Constitution went into effect. The governor's veto was absolute, and he had the power to convene, prorogue, and dissolve the legislature. The delegate to Congress was chosen by the legislature, rather than by the electorate. There were property qualifications for voting and holding office. In later statutes, Congress also specifically reserved the authority to disallow territorial laws. The crucial difference between an English colony and an American territory, of course, was the provisional nature of the latter and the promise of eventual statehood.

Enlightened in its ultimate purpose, but too paternalistic to satisfy self-reliant Westerners, the territorial system underwent changes after 1787 that reflected the general democratic trend of the age. By 1849, when the Territory of Minnesota was organized, the initial, autocratic stage of government had been virtually abandoned. Property qualifications for voting and officeholding had also disappeared. The territorial delegate, both houses of the legislature, and most of the local officers were elected by the people, although the governor remained an appointed federal official. The power of the legislature had been broadened, and with a two-thirds majority, it could now overrule the governor's veto. Yet, while extending self-government with one hand, Congress tightened its hold with the other; for the organic acts became more elaborate and contained lengthening lists of specific restrictions upon territorial authority. Residents of a territory were therefore usually eager for admission to the Union, even though it meant higher tax rates. Local political leaders, their eyes upon the two seats in the United States Senate and other potential prizes, had especially good reasons for pressing toward statehood.

Although Congress enacted some legislation applying to all territories, it did not attempt to make the territorial system absolutely uniform throughout the West. In the state-making process, too, there were many variations and irregularities, but by the 1840s a more or less standard procedure had been installed. It included a congressional enabling act, the calling of a constitutional convention in the territory, submission of the completed state constitution to the territorial electorate, and finally, an act of admission passed by Congress. Down until the Civil War, both the organization of new territories and the admission of new states were often highly controversial issues in American politics. The first major conflict arose over Louisiana, with embittered Federalists arguing that the principle of equal statehood could not lawfully be extended beyond the bounds of the original Union. Beginning with the Missouri struggle of 1819 to 1821, however, it was the slavery question that intruded upon the state-building process, and the resulting entanglement eventually became disastrous for the nation.

Congress extended the territorial system to the Southwest in the 1790s and to Louisiana after its purchase in 1803. New territories were created by subdivision of the original ones as the frontier population increased. Congress shifted boundaries arbitrarily whenever it seemed convenient to do so. In 1800, for example, Northwest Territory was reduced to what is now Ohio and the eastern part of Michigan. The rest of the area became Indiana Territory. The latter, in turn, was diminished in size by the organization of Michigan Territory in 1805 and Illinois Territory in 1809. Wisconsin, before its admission as a state in 1848, had been successively a part of Northwest, Indiana, Illinois, Michigan, and Wisconsin Territories.

The sixteenth state, Tennessee, was the first to enter the Union through the territorial process (1796). Vermont had gained statehood in 1791 by maintaining its independence of New York, and Kentucky had continued to be a county of Virginia until its admission in 1792. State-making north of the Ohio began with Ohio (1803); then Louisiana, which had a head start in population, became the first noncontiguous state (1812). Heavy migration to the Gulf Plains and the lower Ohio Valley produced Indiana (1816), Mississippi (1817), Illinois (1818), and Alabama (1819). The admission of Maine and Missouri followed quickly in 1820 and 1821. After that, there was a considerable pause until Arkansas and Michigan were added to the Union in 1836 and 1837. By this time, most of the Great Plains had been designated "Indian Country," and except for Florida, the only organized territories remaining were in the region north and west of Illinois. The admission of Florida (1845), Iowa (1846), and Wisconsin (1848) even left the United States, for a brief and unique interval, with no organized territories at all. The aggressive expansionism of the 1840s thus coincided with what appeared to be the imminent completion of the state-making process.

THE WESTWARD MIGRATION

Indian removal, land disposal, and the territorial system were all responses of the federal government to the most dynamic element in westward expansion—the spontaneous, disorderly swarming of people along the trails and streams leading into the interior of the continent. This was more than a mere transfer of population; for it meant the birth of new farms and communities, the creation of new markets, and the transplanting of institutions, as well as individuals, to new environments. The westward movement was a social process of an especially fundamental kind because it combined mass migration with the impact of civilization upon the wilderness.

The progress of state-making reflected the general patterns of the westward movement. At first, the major thrust of settlement beyond the Appalachians was heavily concentrated in Kentucky and Tennessee. This may be explained in part by the fact that the parent states of Virginia and North Carolina were among the largest in population at the close of the Revolution. South

Carolina and Georgia had fewer people to contribute to the frontier. As for the more populous states of the north, commercial development was absorbing some of their manpower, and there were still many empty lands available in western New York, northwestern Pennsylvania, and upper New England. Indian resistance also delayed the advance into the Northwest and Southwest during the Federalist period. Thus the settled area of the United States in Jefferson's administration resembled a great triangle with its apex on the Mississippi.

The Ohio River was unrivaled as a highway into the interior, and settlement of the Northwest proceeded northward from its banks. Although New Englanders, Pennsylvanians, and Virginians mingled in Ohio, the early pioneers of Indiana and Illinois were predominantly Southerners coming by way of Kentucky. Their numbers increased rapidly after the War of 1812, but soon the Erie Canal, completed in 1825, had opened a new water route to the West. Then a stream of settlers from New England and the Middle Atlantic states moved into the Lake Plains. Cleveland, Detroit, and Chicago blossomed as lake ports in the 1830s, just as Cincinnati and Louisville had risen on the Ohio River a generation earlier. The population of the upper Northwest was therefore markedly different in origin from that of the Ohio Valley, and a growing influx of European immigrants, especially Germans, further increased the variety of people in the region as a whole. At the same time, the primacy of grain production and related enterprises through-out most of the Northwest made it something of an economic unit de-spite the cultural diversity.

The Southwest, on the other hand, was settled primarily by Southerners engaged in erecting the cotton kingdom. Eli Whitney's simple contrivance for separating seeds from fiber had made large-scale production economically feasible, and the rise of textile manufacture in Europe and America was providing an expansive market for a staple that had been of minor importance during the colonial era. The pressure of soil exhaustion in the South Atlantic states and the attraction of virgin land in the Gulf Plains combined to produce a swelling westward movement of Southerners and cotton production. Only in certain favorable regions, such as the Black Belt of central Alabama and the Mississippi flood plains, did the historic plantation system flourish. Lesser farmers with few or no slaves—the "plain folk" of the South—were the more numerous element in the cotton kingdom, but the large planters set the tone of society and furnished its leadership. The population of the Southwest, relatively homogeneous except for the Negro, developed a distinct class structure even during the frontier phase. Few men in the Northwest were as lordly as the Southern plantation owners, and none were as lowly as the Southern slaves.

The same tasks confronted pioneers of the Northwest and the Southwest when they reached their destinations on the frontier. During the first season, a man usually cleared some ground, planted corn, and erected crude shelters for his family and farm animals. He might dig a well if the nearest stream were not close by, and as winter approached, his need for firewood greatly increased. From such arduous labors, hunting and fishing were welcome

Building a log cabin.

diversions, though very often necessary to supplement the meager store of food. The work of cutting away the forest, digging out stumps, turning over the tough virgin sod, putting up rail fences, and improving the buildings would go on for years. But as soon as possible, the pioneer had to produce something that he could sell for cash and then find a market for it. Corn, wheat, and livestock in the Northwest, cotton and rice in the deep South, and tobacco in the border states—these became the major items of Western agriculture.

The westward movement of the early nineteenth century was an agricultural expansion manned by individual pioneers, but not entirely so. There were also settlers who migrated in organized groups, some of them, like the Mormons and Shakers, bound together by distinctive religious ties. In his heaviest tasks, like house-raising and logrolling, the pioneer often received help from his neighbors, and the plantations of the Southwest functioned more or less like self-contained communities. Villages and towns appeared early in the frontier process, and sometimes, at army forts, trading posts, and river crossings, they actually preceded the development of surrounding farmlands. However, except for a few major ports like Mobile and New Orleans, the Southwest lagged behind in urbanization. In the Northwest, there was a rapid transition from subsistence agriculture to a market economy, with diversification of occupations, rudimentary industry, retail trade, and a consequent proliferation of towns and villages. The westward movement to Illinois, for example, became increasingly a migration of merchants, lawyers, teachers, artisans, and laborers seeking opportunity in a new urban or semiurban environment. On the eve of the Civil War, Illinois stood first among the grain-producing states of the nation, and yet nearly half of the gainfully employed were engaged in pursuits other than farming.

The building of Western society could not be accomplished without financial help from the outside. Frontier churches were often supported by missionary funds collected in the East. Public lands were used to subsidize Western roads and schools. Eastern investors provided much of the capital for Western banks and business enterprises. The bonds of Trans-Appalachian states had to be peddled in the East and in Europe. Probably the most desperate need of the West was for assistance in the improvement of transportation. The need appeared as soon as a region began to produce a substantial surplus that could be sold only in distant markets. This occurred very early in the cotton lands of the Southwest, but there the rivers offered convenient and fairly adequate access to Gulf ports. The grain and livestock

A flatboat on the Mississippi.

producers of the Northwest had larger local markets created by the constant influx of new settlers and the rapid development of nonagricultural enterprise. When this local demand was satisfied, however, the Ohio or Indiana farmer faced a difficult task in disposing of his surplus. At first, he had little choice but to float it down to New Orleans on a flatboat. Then came the steamboat to revolutionize river transportation, while the combination of lake shipping and the Erie Canal provided an outlet to the East Coast. But these very changes increased the need for improved river channels, connecting canals, and lake harbors. Thus the people of the Northwest, equating prosperity with easier access to markets, clamored incessantly for "internal improvements" at public expense.

THE WEST AS A SECTION

When Jefferson became president, the word "West" was generally used to designate all of the country beyond the Appalachians. The Northwest and the Southwest had much in common at first—the experience of conquering the wilderness, the desire for Indian removal and a liberal land policy, the Mississippi River as a highway of commerce. Gradually, however, as the plantation system and its values took root in the Southwest, that region came to be regarded as more Southern than Western. By the 1830s, when men spoke of the "South," they were likely to mean everything from Maryland to Louisiana, whereas farther north, the "West" still began with Ohio. This shifting of the sectional pattern reflected the growing significance of the slavery question as a divisive force in American life.

The Trans-Appalachian region had made its influence felt in national politics as early as the 1780s with demands for free navigation of the Mississippi. Pinckney's Treaty and the Louisiana Purchase, as well as the Land Act of 1800, were responses to the needs of an importunate and growing frontier population. Until 1812, the West was a lesser partner in the victorious coalition forged by Jefferson and Madison, but the influx of new states during the next decade greatly increased Western political power, especially in the Senate. Then, as the rivalry between North and South grew more intense, and the latter expanded to include the slaveholding Western states, the Northwest became plainly the pivotal section in American politics.

In its competition with the Northeast for the allegiance of the Northwest, the South at first had many advantages. Among them were the predominance of Southerners in the settlement of the Ohio Valley, the common interests of primarily agricultural societies, the ties of commerce along the Mississippi River system, and the bond of partnership in the Jeffersonian political synthesis. Federalist New England, after all, had been the most hostile to westward expansion, while the South for a time displayed much sympathy for the needs of the frontier. Calhoun was by no means the only Southerner in 1819 who advocated a broad program of internal improvements. Even as late as 1830, Senator Robert Y. Hayne of South Carolina sprang to the aid of the West on the public lands issue and thereby became engaged in his historic debate with Daniel Webster. Indeed, the political alliance between the South and the older Northwest persisted in certain respects until the eve of the Civil War.

Nevertheless, the two sections were beginning to draw apart by the 1830s. The South, increasingly defensive about slavery as the abolition movement gained momentum, became more of a unit in its insistence upon states' rights and strict construction of the Constitution. This meant that Southerners now offered the most stubborn opposition to internal improvements at federal expense, and in time they also aligned themselves against the Western appeal for free homesteads. Meanwhile, a newer Northwest was arising on the Lake Plains, with a population that looked eastward, rather than southward, to its markets and places of origin. Developing rapidly, this region soon outstripped the older Northwest of the Ohio Valley in agricultural production and political power. By the 1850s, railroad construction and the intensification of the slavery controversy had further strengthened its ties with the Northeast. Thus the Northwest as a whole had itself become somewhat sectionalized and divided in its loyalties, but the preponderant tendency was toward a more "Northern" point of view.

An essential difference between Southern and Western sectionalism was that the latter pressed the federal government for vigorous action, rather than constitutional restraint. The sectional aims of the West were therefore more compatible with nationalism than with states' rights. This fact, together with the slavery issue, largely explains the attitude of the Northwest in the final phase of the sectional controversy. Unlike the Southwest, its ultimate commitment was to the nation.

Chapter IV

The Emerging Age of Enterprise

SEEDTIME OF MODERN AMERICA

From New England farms to Southern plantations, the United States in 1800 was a rural nation. Only 6 percent of its 5 million people lived in towns of 2500 or more, and just two cities (Philadelphia and New York) had populations larger than 50,000. Rural influences pervaded life even in the few urban centers. Agricultural production and agricultural needs provided the major exports, raw materials, and markets of commerce and industry. Townsmen were often part-time farmers, keeping sizable gardens as well as family cows and other livestock.

On the other hand, farm life included many activities besides farming.

Broadway and Park Row in New York City, 1819.

Each rural household was, in some degree, a place of food-processing and manufacture. Butchering and preserving, candlemaking and soapmaking, spinning and weaving, quilting and rugmaking were but a few of the industries carried on in the home. Farmers—together with their families, hired hands, and slaves—did much of their own building. They often worked on local roads and bridges instead of paying taxes for these facilities. They customarily transported their produce to the public market and sold it there themselves. The typical rural American, in short, was a farmer with various secondary occupations. Less than half of the total personal income in the nation came from strictly agricultural pursuits.

Except for the larger towns, all of them seaports, American households and local communities were therefore more or less self-sufficient in 1800. The farmer satisfied most of his own needs or turned to neighboring artisans like the blacksmith, tanner, and cooper. Only occasionally did he visit the nearest general store to obtain things not produced locally, like coffee, salt, hardware, and paint. Barter was common, and relatively little money changed hands. When Jefferson became president, there were but thirty banks in the whole country. Such economic self-reliance meant isolation and provincialism. Poor roads discouraged travel; communication was slow; the post office handled less than one letter per capita during the year. Rural life moved torpidly in narrow, familiar channels.

In the cities the pace was brisker, keyed to a maritime commerce stimulated by the European war. The flourishing merchant marine now totaled a million tons, two-thirds of it engaged in foreign trade. Shipbuilding was a major industry. About a thousand vessels, averaging 100 tons each, were constructed in 1800. Yet American exports and imports amounted, respectively, to only $6 and $10 per capita annually. Foreign trade was the dominant feature of the nation's commerce, but it was of secondary importance in the nation's entire economy. Furthermore, a commercial system oriented primarily to trade with Europe did not intrude significantly upon the repressive localism that separated Americans from one another.

Fifty years later, American society was still predominantly rural. The great expansion into the Mississippi Valley had been primarily agricultural, and the farm population had increased steadily even in the Northeast. According to the census of 1850, more than five-sixths of the 23 million people lived outside the urban communities of 2500 or more. Nearly two-thirds of the labor force was engaged in agriculture. Exports, still about $6 per person annually, were principally farm products, with cotton alone amounting to half of the total. A generation after Jefferson's death, the farmer remained the representative American.

Nevertheless, by 1850 the contours of a vast economic revolution were plainly visible. In some respects it was already well advanced; in others, just beginning. Commercial agriculture had replaced subsistence agriculture in many areas. Local self-sufficiency had given way steadily to specialized production and increased trade. A transportation web of roads and railways, canals and rivers now linked the various parts of the country in a national market.

Industrial growth proceeded at a slower rate than the market revolution, but the foundations of a new economic order had been laid. The factory system was well established in the Northeast. Water wheels and steam engines were providing great new sources of power. Technological progress was accelerating rapidly; the issuance of patents for inventions had multiplied twenty-five times since 1800. The principle of interchangeable parts and the corporate form of business organization were both in use, although the full weight of their revolutionary influence upon industrial production would not be felt until many years after 1850.

The expansion of commerce and industry drew people into towns old and new. Urban population, though still decidedly in the minority, was growing at a much faster rate than the population as a whole. By 1850

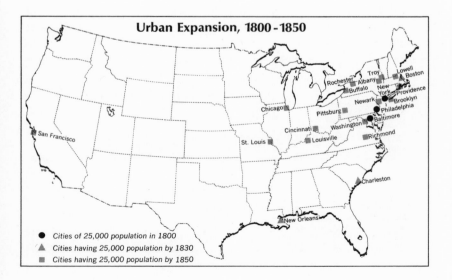

more than a half million persons lived in New York City, and the number of places with at least 10,000 inhabitants had increased from 6 to 62 since 1800. Moreover, the rise of inland cities like Cincinnati, St. Louis, and Chicago reflected the progress of internal trade and Western industry. Urbanization, still in its early stages at mid-century, was another aspect of America's new manifest destiny.

Agriculture, despite the number of people engaged in it, provided less than one-third of the total national income from private production in 1850. Even the farmer was now more or less in business—raising specialized crops for the market, buying goods and services that he once would have supplied himself or done without, borrowing money for capital improvements, and holding his land with an eye to its resale value. Perhaps nothing better indicates the change that came over the United States than the fact that the number of banks increased from about 30 to about 800 in fifty years. The spirit of enterprise, previously confined to a limited group, had become almost universal. Foreign visitors were struck by the economic energy of the American people, by the feverish pursuit of wealth. Alexis de Tocqueville, for example, expressed astonishment at the "innumerable multitude" of small businesses and at the prevalence of "trading passions" in agriculture as well as commerce.

In view of these economic changes, all promising higher productivity, it is surprising to find that the wealth and income of the American people increased more slowly than population during the period from 1800 to 1850. Not until about 1840 did the nation begin to experience the sustained economic growth *per capita* that would be so characteristic of the later nineteenth century. Yet if the upturn seems late, considering the forces at

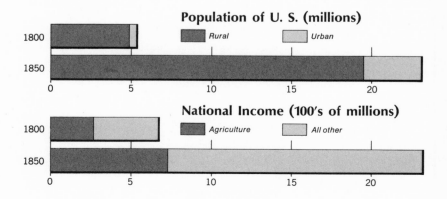

work, it was actually earlier than the standard periodizing of American history has often implied. The secular trend of rising productivity started about two decades before the Civil War, which is commonly used to mark the transition from preindustrial to modern America.

The surge of the American economy after 1840 was, in large measure, the cumulated effect of a revolution that had begun many years earlier. It took time for certain fundamental changes to produce significant results. For example, the application of technology to agriculture apparently did not bring about major increases in total agricultural productivity until about mid-century. And railroad construction, although started in the early 1830s, did not amount to 1000 miles annually until after the Mexican War.

Before 1840, the dynamic elements in the economy were retarded by other factors. The occupation of the Mississippi Valley consumed a vast amount of social energy that was not converted immediately into rising productivity. Household manufacture and subsistence farming, both inefficient modes of production, declined in the East but spread through the frontier West. The spectacular expansion of the cotton kingdom was partly offset by agricultural depression in the older South; and slave labor, though it might be profitable, did not tend to increase per-capita output. Accumulation of capital proceeded at an inadequate rate, impeded by severe financial panics in 1819 and 1837. Improvements in technology and business organization were achieved at the cost of much expensive experimentation and failure.

Thus the era of national expansion was also an era of economic transition. Innovation and enterprise were gradually overcoming the force of tradition, and profound changes were preparing the way for an emerging industrial order. It was a period of preparation for the "take-off" of the American economy.

NEW DIRECTIONS, 1800 TO 1815

The American economy in 1800 was still adjusting to changes wrought by the Revolution. No less than in colonial times, business and urban life were oriented to trade with Europe, but from outside the British imperial system. Independence had meant a loss of commercial privileges that for a time counted more heavily than liberation from the old mercantilistic restrictions. Scrambling for new markets, Yankee merchants sent their ships to the Baltic, the Mediterranean, the Indian Ocean, and across the Pacific to China. These far-flung ventures were exciting and often profitable, but not yet numerous enough to have a significant effect upon the volume of foreign trade.

It was the European war, beginning in 1793, that disrupted the traditional systems of international exchange and enabled the neutral United States to capture a larger part of maritime commerce. Despite the repressive measures of belligerent powers, American seaports bustled with activity, as exports suddenly doubled, the carrying trade flourished, and shipbuilding increased steadily. Most striking of all was the growth of the re-export trade, in which American merchants bought products from one part of the world and sold them to another at a profit. For example, traffic in West Indian sugar multiplied a hundred times during the 1790s.

During these prosperous years at the turn of the century, merchant capitalism reached its final flowering as the dominant form of business organization in the United States. The major mercantile houses of New England and the Middle Atlantic states were usually partnerships or family dynasties. The outstanding characteristic of such firms was the diversity of their operations. They owned and often built their own ships, traded at home and abroad as both wholesalers and retailers, handled goods for other merchants, loaned money and otherwise acted as bankers, assumed the risks of marine insurance, and sometimes also engaged in manufacturing. But by 1815, although versatile merchant kings like John Jacob Astor were still the most prominent figures on the scene, a general trend toward the separation of business functions had set in. More and more firms tended to concentrate on just one or two of the many activities that the merchant capitalist had encompassed. Insurance, for example, became an enterprise in itself, and exporters shipped their goods increasingly by common carriers. In the business world, as in other segments of the economy, the jack-of-all-trades was giving way to the specialist.

The flush times lasted until 1807, but then Jefferson's Embargo and the War of 1812 played havoc with America's swollen foreign trade. Idle ships in every port signified a maritime depression. On the other hand, the sharp reduction of imports stimulated domestic industry. Household manufacturing, especially of textiles, expanded greatly, while the gains of handicraft and factory production for the market were more modest. Some of the capital and labor previously invested in foreign commerce now found its way into industry. The Embargo and the British blockade served the purpose of a protective tariff, turning American enterprise inward, away from the sea. The total effect was less than revolutionary, for these trends were partially reversed after 1815 when foreign trade revived and manufacturers faced renewed competition from abroad. Nevertheless, Americans had made long strides toward the development of a domestic market and a more balanced economy.

Meanwhile, the winds of change were blowing through the agricultural South. The tobacco plantations of tidewater Virginia and Maryland showed the sad effects of depressed prices and depleted soils. Tobacco continued to be an important market crop in the Piedmont region of North Carolina and southern Virginia, as well as in Kentucky and certain other Western states, but it had lost its prime position in the Southern economy. The financial distress of Jefferson and Madison during their later years symbolized the decline of Virginia and its great staple from their proud eminence in Revolutionary times.

Farther south, the tidewater economy remained more stable. The rice plantations of South Carolina and Georgia continued to prosper, and although the foreign market for indigo had long since collapsed, cotton was taking its place as a second staple. However, rice and long-staple cotton could be raised only along the coast. Neither offered much potential for expansion. Short-staple cotton, which required only good soil, adequate rainfall, and a fairly long growing season, was unprofitable as long as the separation of seeds from fiber had to be done by hand.

Eli Whitney's invention of the cotton gin in 1793 solved this vexing problem and set the stage for a revolution. Production increased tenfold during the decade that followed. Cotton was well suited to slave labor, and markets at home and abroad were expanding rapidly as the textile industry gathered momentum. Originating in the back country of South Carolina and Georgia, the cotton kingdom spread northward as far as southwestern Virginia and westward into the virgin lands of the Tennessee Valley and the Gulf Coastal Plain. By 1815, the crop had already become the most dynamic element in the nation's changing economy.

The great historical significance of cotton resulted primarily from the fact that it was a cash crop in an increasingly money-conscious age. Actually, the South as a whole raised more corn than cotton right down to the Civil War. But most of the corn was consumed locally by humans and animals. Cotton went entirely into the market, stimulating the flow of trade. As early as the 1820s, cotton planters were supplying nearly half of all American exports in value and, at the same time, providing domestic industry with its most important raw material.

Thus, when the War of 1812 ended, both the North and the South were already undergoing radical economic changes that would soon be accelerated by the rush of settlers into the Mississippi Valley. A nation hitherto predominantly maritime in its outlook was now ready for intensive exploitation of a continent.

THE TRANSPORTATION REVOLUTION

Correlative with the mass movement into the West and the growth of national markets after 1815 was a series of revolutionary developments in transportation. Here, technological innovation had its most dramatic effect upon American life, and the spirit of enterprise achieved its boldest expression.

For the coastal regions from New England to Louisiana, the sea remained the principal highway. The American merchant marine entered its greatest period of sustained expansion after 1815, and coasting vessels were a steadily increasing percentage of the total tonnage. The leading item of trade was cotton, shipped from Gulf ports to Northeastern cities, but out of New Orleans went a variety of products that had come down the Mississippi. On the return voyage, ships usually carried manufactured goods of both American and European origin. An innovation of major importance was the packet line, operating on a regular schedule. Steamships made their appearance in the 1820s, but they did not replace the sailing vessels; for the latter continued to dominate the coasting trade until after the Civil War.

Steam power had a much more immediate and decisive influence upon transportation in the interior regions. There, except on the Great Lakes, sailing vessels were of limited use, and the flatboats, barges, and keelboats moved with distressing slowness toward their destinations. Soon after the success of Robert Fulton's *Clermont* in 1807, steamboats began to appear on Western waters. As they eventually developed, with their considerable speed, flat bottoms, incredibly shallow drafts, and their lofty and often ornate superstructures, these floating wooden buildings were admirably suited for river navigation. The steamboat made upstream travel easy for the first time, and it greatly increased the volume and velocity of trade. Enhancing the

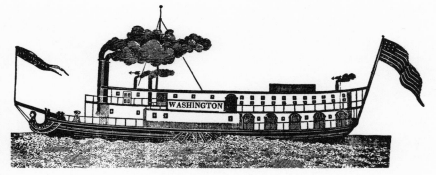

A woodcut of the steamboat *Washington,* built at Cincinnati in 1820.

importance of New Orleans and other river cities, and adding a new and colorful unit to American culture, it became the dominant symbol of inland commercial progress.

The South and West relied all the more heavily upon river transportation because their roads were so inadequate. Although local country roads remained primitive everywhere, a network of more or less improved highways connected the Atlantic states by 1815. This was the era of turnpikes, like the admirable thoroughfare of gravel on a stone foundation that ran from Philadelphia to Lancaster, Pennsylvania. Privately financed and collecting tolls, turnpikes proved in the end to be unprofitable investments, and by the 1830s they were withering away. Roadbuilding by state governments was desultory at best, while ambitious plans for an extensive federal system of internal improvements ran afoul of constitutional scruples and sectional antagonisms. The most important highway into the West, however, was the National Road, built with funds received from the sale of federal lands. Starting at Cumberland on the upper Potomac, it reached Wheeling in 1818 and Columbus in 1833. Construction across Indiana was not completed until 1850, and by then much of the project had been turned over to the states. Stagecoach and mail service improved wherever good roads were built, but wagon freighting continued to be very expensive in comparison with water transportation.

While New Orleans prospered as the outlet of the Mississippi and its tributaries, Eastern states pondered ways of piercing the Appalachian barrier and tapping the trade of the growing West. New York acted first and with the greatest success by constructing the Erie Canal between 1817 and 1825.

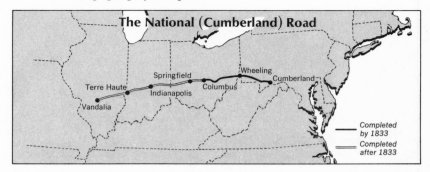

Extending 363 miles from the Hudson River to Lake Erie, this project was a monumental undertaking for its time. It cost $7 million, but the tolls amounted to more than that in the first ten years of operation. The Canal speeded the development not only of western New York but of the whole Great Lakes region beyond. It diverted the trade of the upper Northwest from New Orleans to New York City and made the latter supreme among Atlantic seaports. Probably no other single achievement in transportation had such decisive effects upon American history.

New York's bold venture started a boom in canal-building that lasted about a generation. Between 1815 and 1840, more than 3000 miles of artificial waterways were constructed in the United States, at a total cost of $125 million. State governments supplied a major part of the capital, and several of them were brought to the verge of bankruptcy by their extravagance. One notable effort to compete with the Erie was the cumbersome Pennsylvania "Main Line," a combination of canals and railroads running from Philadelphia to Pittsburgh. Along the Atlantic coast, a number of waterways were built to improve water travel between the tidewater and back country. The canal enthusiasm also swept into Ohio and other states of the Northwest. There the principal object was to link the Great Lakes with the Ohio-Mississippi system. Although some of these projects were successful, they left the state governments staggering under the burden of debts. The Panic of 1837 and the increasing competition from railroads soon brought the canal-building era to an end.

The most revolutionary innovation of all was the steam railroad, which made its appearance about 1830. Within a decade, more than 3000 miles of track were in operation, and it had become clear that the locomotive would conquer the continent. Here at last was a means of transportation

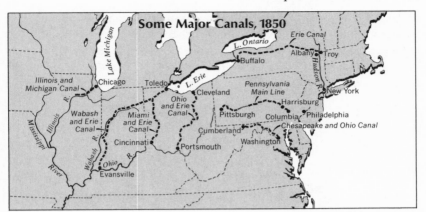

One of the earliest American locomotives, purchased in England for the Delaware and Hudson Company.

on land that rivaled the speed and convenience of ocean-going vessels. The railroads broke the bonds of nature; for they could cross ridges, penetrate regions remote from navigable waterways, and provide service throughout the frozen months of winter. The first lines were built in the Atlantic states, but the enthusiasm spread quickly into the West. By the late 1840s a railroad

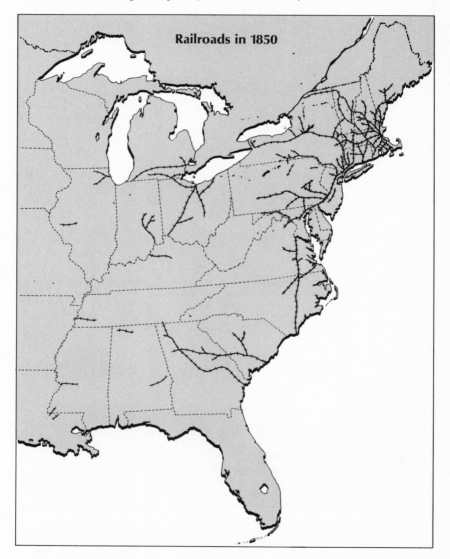

Railroads in 1850

boom was well under way, and a transportation network had begun to take shape.

Although some states built their own railroads, the standard method of organization came to be the chartered corporation, using private capital, but depending heavily upon public assistance in the form of subscriptions to stock, subsidies, and various special privileges. The American economy was at first more powerfully affected by the promotion and construction of railroads than by their actual operation. Except in the Northeast, the railroad by 1850 had just begun to have its revolutionary influence upon transportation and trade.

Until the 1840s, communication improved no faster than the best transportation, but then Samuel F. B. Morse demonstrated the efficiency and utility of his electric telegraph. No major invention of the time was put more speedily into use. Relatively easy and cheap to install, telegraph wires crisscrossed the eastern half of the country by the early 1850s, and a transcontinental line was completed during the first year of the Civil War. Thus the telegraph, like the steamboat and railroad, made an expanding nation in some respects smaller.

POWER, TECHNOLOGY, AND THE CORPORATION

Men like Morse were the Eastern counterparts of Western explorers. Their realm of adventure was the "intensive frontier" of science, technology, and business organization. Instead of new lands, they sought new ways of getting things done. Innovation, no less than expansion, was the spirit of the age, and innovators were the pioneers of the industrial revolution.

Greater concentrations of power were indispensable for large-scale industrial production. Here, the most important change in the early nineteenth century was not the invention of something utterly new, but rather the progressive, unspectacular improvement of a familiar device. The awkward water mills of colonial times, although ubiquitous, were of limited capacity and were used only on small streams. Beginning in the 1790s, larger and more complex installations in sizable rivers greatly increased the amount of power available to manufacturing communities. Metal gears and leather belts made transmission more efficient, and by 1850 the hydraulic turbine had started to replace the water wheel. Before the days of electricity, however, water power could not be transmitted any distance from its source. As a consequence, factory towns were necessarily river towns, clustered especially on the fall lines of Eastern states.

Except in transportation, the influence of the steam engine was less than revolutionary before the Civil War. Relatively expensive to install and operate, it did not easily replace the water wheel. Steam power appeared most rapidly in regions like the Ohio Valley where water power was unreliable and in industries like ironmaking that required heat. The mobility and versatility of the steam engine were among its greatest advantages. By 1850, many newspaper presses, fire engines, and cotton gins were operating on steam. For large-scale manufacturing, however, water remained the principal source of power.

The development of water and steam power was but one aspect of technological change along a broad front, produced by a whole army of lesser innovators and adapters, as well as those inventors whose names have been recorded in history books. The conquest of successive frontiers had accustomed Americans to the challenge of new problems. Even though many people were slow to accept innovations, a general scarcity of labor in relation to exploitable natural resources encouraged experiments with labor-saving devices and techniques. The comparative weakness of the European craft tradition in the United States probably fostered technological adventuring, and so did a generous patent system which provided financial protection for inventors.

American technology in the nineteenth century was almost invariably pragmatic—the response of ingenuity to immediate needs, rather than a systematic application of scientific knowledge. The typical inventor had less formal learning than practical skill, less interest in testing theories than in solving specific problems. Furthermore, the technological revolution in its earlier stages was associated primarily with the production and exchange of goods. Patterns of consumption in the average home changed more slowly than industrial and agricultural methods. The American kitchen, for example, remained relatively primitive. Only recently has it become a showplace and symbol of material progress.

The catalog of technological changes in the first half of the nineteenth century included more efficient spinning and weaving machines, the puddling process and rolling mills in the iron industry, screw propulsion on steamships, the reaper and thresher, the vulcanizing of rubber, the cylinder printing press, improved animal breeding, and the use of anesthetics in medicine. But perhaps the most important items of all were the machine tools (like the power lathe), used in the making of other machines. Heavily dependent at first upon Britain, the United States by mid-century was becoming a world leader in the designing and manufacture of specialized machine tools. Meanwhile, in the firearms industry, a uniquely American contribution to technology had appeared. This was the precision manufacture of interchangeable parts, a revolutionary development that eventually became the basis for modern mass production.

Technology tended to enlarge the scale of enterprise and thus to require greater concentrations of capital than individual proprietors and simple partnerships could readily provide. One result was an increasing dependence upon credit among entrepreneurs of every sort, including farmers. Another was the evolution of more sophisticated forms of business organization. The chartered corporation and the unchartered joint-stock company, both quite rare before 1800, were well suited to the needs of the new industrial era. By the sale of shares, large numbers of investors could be drawn into a single enterprise, while the transferability of ownership lent permanence to a company and gave it an independent identity.

The corporation usually had additional advantages conferred by its charter. Most important was limited liability, which meant that a shareholder risked no more than his investment. This principle, although slow to win adoption in some states, eventually became a standard feature of corporations and made it easier to attract capital. Used in the beginning primarily by banks, insurance firms, canal builders, and land speculators, the corporate system spread gradually into manufacturing and commerce. At first, each charter required a special legislative act, but by the 1840s, there was a definite trend toward general laws setting the standards and procedures for incorporation. This removed much of the odor of monopoly from the device and made it available to all groups that could meet the legal requirements. By separating ownership from control and facilitating the concentration of capital for large-scale enterprise, the corporation provided the organizational means for the emergence of "big business" after the Civil War.

FINANCING ECONOMIC EXPANSION

The growth of a market economy rapidly increased the volume of commercial transactions, thereby producing great new demands for money and credit. Closely related was the mounting need for capital to support enterprises requiring substantial investment. In response to absolute necessity, there developed a cluster of practices and institutions that can only loosely be termed a financial "system." This system, which was the work of private initiative and public policy (both state and federal), matched the disorderliness but also the energy of the young American nation.

Money as a medium of exchange had long been a serious problem because the supply of gold and silver in the country was chronically inadequate. Furthermore, in contrast to the Revolutionary era, the federal government now generally refrained from issuing paper money, and the Constitution forbade state governments to do so. At the same time, even a completely satisfactory currency would not have altered the importance of credit, especially in a nation with pronounced seasonal cycles of trade. The farmer often needed things in the spring that he could not pay for until fall. The merchant often needed to replenish his stock of goods before he had received full payment for sales already made. Commercial credit, usually a short-term arrangement, facilitated trade and increased its velocity. Such credit was continually liquidated and renewed in the chain of transactions between producer and consumer. No less essential and more difficult to obtain was the long-term credit required for the exploitation of new lands, the construction of transportation facilities, and the launching of industrial enterprises.

Actually, a good deal of money was improvised. Warehouse receipts, promissory notes, private scrip, state treasury notes (in violation of the Constitution), and other nondescript paper often circulated freely. Since most of these informal currencies were simply promises to pay, they served a dual purpose as instruments of credit and mediums of exchange. Credit, like money, took many forms. Much of it was arranged privately and directly by the principals—that is, by individuals and business firms. Thus the functions of banking were not left exclusively to chartered banks. Nevertheless, the latter became increasingly important as sources of both currency and credit.

Bankers were in some degree middlemen who received funds for deposit and loaned them at interest. But a bank could also "create" money by granting a loan and then crediting the amount of it to the borrower's account, without using any cash. This was done in the knowledge that not all deposits would be withdrawn at one time. In addition, banks created money by issuing their own notes and paying them out instead of specie as much as possible. These bank notes were merely promises to pay upon demand, but ordinarily

A three-dollar bank note issued in Michigan.

only a fraction of them would be presented regularly for conversion to gold or silver. The rest circulated and served as the most common form of paper currency in the country. Since a bank's lending power and profits depended heavily upon the amount of such paper that it could keep in circulation, some institutions made it a practice to distribute their notes far from home. An inaccessible location also discouraged the return of notes to the issuing corporation. Those deep in the backwoods and hardest to reach were called "wildcat" banks.

A bank had to keep a certain amount of specie on hand for redemption of its notes, and this reserve ratio was often fixed by law. A notable example of stringent regulation was the Louisiana statute of 1842 which required a specie reserve equal to one-third of all note and deposit liabilities. But in deflationary periods, even the most conservative banks were hard pressed and might have to suspend specie payments. Sometimes, as a result, an institution became bankrupt; more often its notes continued to circulate at a discount until business improved and specie payments could be resumed. Indeed, during good times as well as bad, many bank notes lacked full public confidence and therefore commanded less than their face value in financial transactions. The great variety of such notes with different and fluctuating values was a chronic nuisance for businessmen, who also had to be on guard against fraudulent and counterfeit issues. In the major cities, "bank note detectors" were published for their guidance. Because of the close relation between note circulation and credit expansion, efforts at stricter regulation of the former tended to impede the latter and drew protests from borrowers. An unstable currency and, in some degree, the financial panics of 1819 and 1837 were part of the price that Americans paid for a credit system suited to their needs.

Across the country, banking organization took various forms and underwent continual change. Some banks were virtually public agencies, controlled and partly financed by state governments. Although the constitutionality of such institutions and their note issues seemed dubious, it was upheld by the Supreme Court in *Briscoe v. The Bank of Kentucky* (1837). At the same time, certain states permitted no banking at all. Others chartered privately financed institutions in limited numbers. An influential New York act, passed in 1838, authorized any group of citizens who met specified requirements to establish a bank. Like general incorporation laws, this "free banking" system reflected the spirit of competitive enterprise, and other states soon imitated it.

Regulation of banking was not left entirely to government. Larger banks, alone or in combination, often exercised considerable influence on the credit and note-issuing policies of smaller institutions with which they did business. Beginning in the 1820s, for example, the Suffolk Bank and other Boston banks established a system of control that extended throughout New England. This amounted to central banking on a regional basis. At the national level, however, only the Bank of the United States had enough power to attempt such a role.

From 1791 to 1811, the First Bank of the United States had functioned as a major commercial bank and bank of issue, as the fiscal agent of the federal government, and in some degree as a central bank, regulating the note circulation of other institutions by insisting upon redeemability. Its successor, chartered in 1816, got off to a bad start and averted disaster only by a policy of drastic retrenchment that helped precipitate the Panic of 1819. During the presidency of Nicholas Biddle, which began in 1823, the Second Bank became increasingly prosperous and powerful. But then Andrew Jackson vetoed the bill for renewal of its charter, and the Bank ceased to be a federal institution. After 1836, as a consequence, the field of commercial banking and note issue was left to the multiplying state banks, while the United States assumed management of its own fiscal affairs through the subtreasury system. As for central banking, it had been set aside for the rest of the century.

Commercial banks were primarily a source of short-term mercantile credit, although in rural areas they also made mortgage loans for longer periods. The capital needed for industrial expansion and transportation development came ultimately from people with savings to lend or invest, but it reached the users in a variety of ways. Commercial banks, savings banks, and insurance companies all participated in the process. In addition, lotteries were a common means of raising money for public and private projects. Increasingly, however, it was by the sale of government and corporate securities that savings were converted into investment. The marketing of stocks and bonds at home and abroad became a specialized business, and along with this investment banking there developed stock exchanges for trading in securities. No single city monopolized these activities, but New York gradually assumed the place of leadership.

INDUSTRIAL ENTERPRISE

Household manufacturing, the most widespread form of industry at the beginning of the nineteenth century, declined in importance after 1815. It survived wherever isolation discouraged trade, and it retreated from the advancing lines of transportation. Hence the change took place more rapidly in the East than in the West. Many items that the American consumer had once made for himself or had done without now came increasingly from abroad, from expanding handicraft production, and from the emerging factory system.

In this early stage of the industrial revolution, the transitional figure was the craftsman. Having always produced goods for sale, he adjusted readily to the demands and opportunities of a market economy, but not without assuming a somewhat different role. Instead of making hats or shoes to order for specific customers, the craftsman began turning out ready-made products for the general public. Very often, he ceased to do his own retailing and dealt only with merchants. If business prospered, he enlarged his shop, hired additional journeymen and apprentices, and gave more time to supervision and less to work at his own bench. With the development of transportation and trade, certain crafts tended to concentrate in a few communities. Danbury, Connecticut, became famous, for example, as a hatmaking center. Eventually, the application of power and machine technology to such handicraft complexes would convert them into factory systems, but that occurred chiefly after 1850.

In the manufacture of shoes, textiles, and certain other items, the "domestic" or "putting-out" system was extensively used. Here the entrepreneur, whether merchant or master craftsman, provided the raw materials and general management for work performed in the home. The labor involved might require considerable skill, but often it was so simple that the whole family could take part. Although the domestic system lasted for many years in some industries, it served primarily as an intermediate stage in the transition from household and handicraft manufacture to factory production.

The factory system, developing gradually and unevenly, did not become typical of American industry until after the Civil War, but it had begun to emerge early in the nineteenth century. The word "factory" implies integrated production of standardized goods for a mass market, using power-driven machinery and relatively large numbers of hired workers assembled under one roof. The first significant appearance of these characteristics was in the cotton mills of New England, where water power, capital, and an adequate labor force were all available.

Although spinning mills dated from the 1790s, the first real textile factory was organized in 1813 at Waltham, Massachusetts, by Francis C. Lowell and other wealthy Bostonians. Introducing the power loom, they brought together in one plant all the primary cotton-manufacturing processes—spinning, weaving, bleaching, dyeing, and printing. The company produced a standardized inexpensive cloth for which there were rapidly expanding markets at home and abroad. Needing low-priced labor of no great skill, the owners recruited farm girls and built dormitories to house them. The Waltham system proved so successful that its promoters eventually established factories in a number of New England towns, and many other enterprisers imitated their example.

At varying rates of speed, the principal elements of the factory system were adopted in a number of industries, including glass, woolen goods, and firearms. Large urban flour mills became veritable factories; so did some tanneries, distilleries, and cabinetmaking firms. Yet the same products were also turned out by many small neighborhood enterprises scattered across the country. Mass-production methods dominated few industries before the Civil War. In 1850, there were about 125,000 manufacturing establishments, employing an average of only eight workers per unit.

The most basic industry of all was ironmaking, important even in colonial times, but transformed by the ever-increasing demands of the new machine age. Iron production in the eighteenth century had been typically a modest enterprise, using nearby ore deposits and serving a local, rural market. Refining was usually a two-step process, first in a blast furnace, then in an open forge—both heated with charcoal. Shortly after the War of 1812, rolling mills began to replace trip hammers in the shaping of bar iron. The next major innovation was the puddling process, which used a closed furnace instead of a forge to refine the pig iron. This method kept the metal separated from the fuel and made it possible to substitute coal for charcoal. With these changes and concurrent improvements in transportation, iron-making tended to become a large-scale urban enterprise, although much of the ore was still being smelted in charcoal-burning blast furnaces widely dispersed throughout the countryside. The movement of the blast furnaces into the cities and their conversion to coal began as early as the 1830s, but occurred largely after the Civil War. Although considerable quantities of iron were manufactured in many parts of the nation, by 1850 about one-half of the industry was concentrated in Pennsylvania, where anthracite mines supplied the best kind of fuel.

THE WORKING CLASS

The market revolution and the emergence of the factory system not only increased the number of wage earners at a rapid rate but greatly altered the character and conditions of their work. As enterprises grew larger, there was a decline in the personal relationship between employers and the people whom they hired. Standardized production meant standardized performance, with the worker putting little of his unique self into the impersonal process. Labor tended to become faceless, something to be bought in the market along with raw materials and capital goods.

From 1815 to 1850, daily wages for male millhands and other laborers averaged about 75 cents to $1. Skilled workers received more; women and children, considerably less. These amounts are misleading unless we remember that a dollar would buy perhaps ten pounds of meat or several gallons of whiskey or almost an acre of public land. Often the employee received his wages in depreciated paper currency or in orders on a company store. Work days, even for children, were usually twelve to thirteen hours long. There was little protection against injuries and illness, or against the wage reductions and lay-offs that came with hard times.

The conditions of the working class in America nevertheless compared favorably with those in Europe. Industrial expansion and the constant flow of the westward movement kept labor relatively scarce, although the increasing volume of immigration after 1830 did tend to heighten the competition for jobs and thus hold wage levels down. Furthermore, the average working-man expected eventually to improve his economic status, and young women generally regarded industrial employment as an interlude before marriage. There was no permanent class of hired workers in the country, said Abraham Lincoln. "The man who labored for another last year, this year labors for himself, and next year he will hire others to labor for him." Social mobility in America, a potent blend of reality and myth, discouraged the development of class-conscious labor solidarity.

Early factory workers occasionally made crude efforts to organize and even staged a few strikes, but these were always temporary responses to immediate grievances. Organization on a more permanent basis began in the crafts like shoemaking, carpentry, and printing. These craftsmen had a long tradition of guildlike association. In the new age of expanding markets and industrialized production, they were threatened not only with loss of status but with pressure for lower wages. Craft societies therefore multiplied and became more aggressive. Using collective bargaining and the strike, they sought to obtain better pay, shorter hours, and the closed shop. Trade-union activity reached a peak in the 1830s. By then, some degree of horizontal and vertical federation had been achieved. In certain larger cities, there were central councils of the various local trades, and some crafts had organized national unions. The next step was the formation of a National Trades' Union in 1834. This first attempt to organize all craftsmen on a national scale soon ended in failure; for the Panic of 1837 swept away most of the trade-union structure in the United States. Rebuilding had to begin at the local level, and not until the 1850s did national organizations again appear.

Employers were not slow in forming their own associations to resist the trade-union movement, and they often drew upon the courts for assistance. Beginning as early as 1805, a number of judicial decisions held that union activity was a criminal conspiracy in restraint of trade under the common law. As social consciousness became more pronounced, a revulsion set in against this severe doctrine. In *Commonwealth v. Hunt* (1842), the highest court of Massachusetts upheld the right of workers to organize, and the case was widely accepted as a precedent. Nevertheless, law enforcement continued to be weighted in favor of the employer for many years thereafter.

Along with efforts at organization and collective bargaining, workers also pursued their objectives through political action. Elimination of property qualifications for voting enfranchised many urban laborers, and by the late 1820s workingmen's parties were springing up in a number of states. They won some modest victories, but some of them found that it was more profitable to operate within the ranks of a major party. In New York and Massachusetts, for example, the workingmen became an influential wing of Jacksonian Democracy.

The membership of workingmen's political organizations were usually heterogeneous, including craftsmen, shopkeepers, professional men, and farmers. Their objectives consequently tended to be much broader than those of the trade unions. They demanded better public school systems and the abolition of imprisonment for debt. They were hostile to banks and in favor of free homesteads for Western settlers. In short, they became a part of the general movement for social reforms aimed at uplifting the common man. Such humanitarian purposes even carried some workingmen into Fourierism and other utopian schemes of the day. As a result, their attention was distracted for a time from the task of rebuilding the labor organizations destroyed by the Panic of 1837.

GOVERNMENT AND THE ECONOMY

The remarkable growth and transformation of the American economy during the first half of the nineteenth century was largely the work of private enterprise, but this does not mean that government assumed a passive role. The golden age of laissez-faire is one of the great historical myths, fashioned in later years by men who wove their own dogmas into the fabric of the past. Jeffersonian theorists were indeed hostile to concentration of political power in the national capital, and Jacksonian Democrats denounced the use of public authority to sustain privilege and monopoly. Yet few Americans subscribed to the doctrine of minimal government at all levels and in all circumstances. On the contrary, believing that the state was their servant, the people repeatedly invoked its aid in the economic development of the country.

The national economy was strongly affected by various policies of the federal government—notably in banking, tariff legislation, and disposal of the public domain. Also, the United States operated the Post Office, one of the largest and most essential enterprises in the country; it built the National Road and the first telegraph line; it subsidized canals, steamship companies, and eventually railroads; it provided social insurance and hospitals for sick and disabled seamen; until 1822, it maintained a string of Indian trading posts as a public business; and for a variety of private producers, like arms manufacturers, it was a major customer. These activities all fell within a rather narrow range, but the limits were set by the constitutional principle of federalism, rather than the economic doctrine of laissez-faire.

It was at the state and local level that government assumed broad responsibilities in economic affairs. Extensive community regulation of innkeeping, marketing, breadmaking, and many other activities dated back to the colonial period. The growth of trade and industry in the nineteenth century created additional needs for regulatory action, and since the problems were no longer local, the primary burden fell upon the states. The power to issue charters gave state governments a special kind of control over banking and other corporate enterprise, but the state police power reached into virtually every field of economic activity. For instance, the state acted as regulator by licensing trades and professions, setting standards of quality, providing for inspection of products, and defining the relationships between creditor and debtor.

At the same time, state governments were strenuously endeavoring to promote economic progress. By means of bounties, tax exemptions, and other subsidies, they lent support to a wide variety of interests. The states also engaged directly in mixed enterprises; that is, they supplied part of the capital for certain corporations. More than that, they completely owned and operated some of the biggest enterprises, such as canals and early railroads. Schools and roads became increasingly a public responsibility during this period. Thus the state governments regulated business, promoted business, and engaged in business, as the circumstances seemed to require. Many of their efforts were badly managed, and some ended in utter failure, but then the record of private enterprise was not one of unbroken successes either.

By the 1840s, there were indeed signs of a reaction against government intervention in economic affairs. The sad experience of some states in their internal-improvement programs had been disillusioning. More private capital was now available, while state treasuries and state credit were badly depleted. In addition, the ideas of Adam Smith and British classical economists had begun to make headway among American intellectuals. From this point on, the principle of laissez-faire gained adherents and a measure of public acceptance, but neither in theory nor in practice was it typical of early nineteenth century America.

Chapter V

The Jacksonian Republic

THE MOLD OF POLITICS IN THE 1820s

As the fiftieth anniversary of Independence drew near, the United States showed many signs of political stability. Born of revolution, the nation had not been shaken by any serious uprisings. Transfers of power were accomplished more or less peacefully in regular elections. Patriotic feeling and national self-confidence ran high. The American people had a lustrous history to celebrate and a roll of heroes to honor, from the Father of his Country to the Victor of New Orleans. Despite the doubts of some theorists, the republican system of government had proved adaptable to a large and expanding domain. The federal Constitution, last amended in 1804, would remain unchanged until after the Civil War. In the states, there was much more revising of fundamental law, but the alterations tended to produce a greater amount of uniformity. At each level of government, customary forms and procedures, as well as a modest bureaucracy, lent continuity to the political order.

Yet the 1820s may also be viewed as an interval of turbulent transition from the old republic of the founders to the spirited, disorderly, and volatile democratic republic of the nineteenth century. Three major changes in progress were the democratizing of political institutions, the emergence of definite sectional alignments in national politics, and the erection of a new two-party system.

Political democracy had been gaining ground steadily since the Revolution. It was not a sudden achievement of the Jacksonian period. The trend toward universal white manhood suffrage began in many states with the elimination of religious tests and the substitution of taxpaying for propertyholding qualifications. The next step was the abandonment of the taxpaying requirement, leaving residence, age, sex, race, and in some cases citizenship as the bases of enfranchisement. These changes were accomplished, however, by each state at its own pace and in its own manner. Ohio, for example, established a taxpaying qualification in 1801 and kept it for half a century, while New York clung to its freehold requirements until 1828, but retained taxpaying as a substitute for only five years thereafter. As early as 1777, Vermont had framed a constitution containing no propertyholding or taxpaying limitations upon the right to vote; yet it did include a religious test for officeholders. Virginia renounced religious qualifications at an early date, but did not grant manhood suffrage until 1851. Although new Western states generally favored liberal suffrage laws, their progress in this direction was not conspicuously ahead of the Eastern seaboard.

With landowning fairly common in early America, the removal of property qualifications had something less than a revolutionary effect on the political system. Furthermore, there were some important exceptions to the liberal trend. The number of states extending suffrage to free Negroes actually declined, even while the antislavery movement was gathering momentum. New Jersey, which had permitted some widows to vote, withdrew the privilege in 1807, thus making the exclusion of women universal throughout the country. The widespread policy of letting aliens vote was bitterly attacked by nativist elements, although without much success before the Civil War. Yet, despite its limitations, liberalization of the franchise did signal the advance of democratic principles along a broad front.

The gradual adoption of the written ballot was generally regarded as a democratic victory, since the poorer voters had allegedly been subject to intimidation under the older *viva-voce* system. More state and local offices became elective, and in most states the selection of presidential electors was transferred from the legislature to the people. These changes likewise occurred gradually, but they were well under way by the 1820s. The same decade saw the end of the congressional caucus as the method of nominating presidential candidates. It was replaced in the 1830s by the national party convention, which added drama as well as democracy to the quadrennial campaigns. The convention system spread rapidly into state and local politics, making each party organization a loose hierarchy of representative assemblies. Meanwhile, the separation of church and state had been completed when Massachusetts at last disestablished the Congregational Church in 1833. Furthermore, as literacy increased with educational progress, and as party newspapers multiplied throughout the country, public interest in politics

The Capitol in Washington, D. C., 1827.

became broader and more intense. Foreign visitors were usually astonished at the interminable discussions of candidates and issues, and at the feverish excitement that accompanied campaigns and elections. It was the growing enthusiasm for political activity, as well as the trend toward manhood suffrage, that made this preeminently the age of democracy.

Sectionalism, always a factor in national politics, became more potent after 1820. The sudden transformation of John C. Calhoun from an ardent nationalist into an architect of nullification dramatized the fact that the South had replaced New England as the stronghold of particularism and strict constitutionalism. Sectional rivalry during the 1820s revolved primarily about the tariff question, but it was slavery, above all, that identified the South and burdened its people with a growing sense of insecurity. More viable than ever since the rise of cotton culture, the institution was also plainly becoming more vulnerable. The Missouri controversy had alerted Southerners to the strength of antislavery feeling in the North, and soon they would experience the fierce assaults of organized abolitionism. No less disturbing was the fear of slave insurrections, which seldom materialized but were frequently rumored. These pressures produced solidarity where there once had been considerable diversity and doubt. The South choked back its earlier apologies and began to invoke religion, history, and science in defense of slavery as a good and permanent institution. For a quarter of a century after 1820, the commitment was put to only limited tests, but in the background it constantly molded Southern political behavior.

Of course this does not mean that the South consistently acted as a unit in national politics. Southeastern and Southwestern Congressmen might stand together against a protective tariff, but they usually parted company when the discussion turned to internal improvements or public land policies. Sections, after all, were vague geographic entities having no legal existence, and sectional loyalty competed with other loyalties that also influenced political action. Each major section was a complex of subsections, states, and localities with diverse and often conflicting interests. At the same time, sectional differences were frequently transcended by national patriotism, by party allegiance, and by intersectional bargaining. Sectionalism, in short, was neither simple as a pattern nor unremitting and absolute as a commitment. Nevertheless, during the 1820s it became an increasingly powerful crosscurrent in the stream of politics.

The 1820s also proved to be a critical period in the history of American political parties. The only comparable decade is the 1850s. In both cases, the death of one major party was followed by an interval of multiparty or multifactional activity and then by restoration of the two-party system. This analogy will not bear much weight, however; for the circumstances and events that produced the age of Jackson were in many respects unique.

ADAMS AND JACKSON

The Republican party, having eliminated its Federalist opposition, began to break into factions. Whereas Monroe had been the only candidate in the perfunctory election of 1820, four contestants scrambled for the presidency in 1824. William H. Crawford of Georgia, the Southern favorite, suffered a paralytic stroke but remained in the race. Supporters of the distinguished and austere John Quincy Adams were concentrated largely in New England and New York. Henry Clay's center of strength was the Ohio Valley. Only Andrew Jackson had significant support in more than one section, but many political leaders considered this fierce military chieftain unfit for the office. A fifth candidate, John C. Calhoun, had withdrawn from the contest and agreed to accept the vice-presidency.

In the election, no candidate won a majority of the electoral votes. Jackson received the largest number, and Adams was close behind him. Crawford finished third, slightly ahead of Clay. This meant that the House of Representatives, with one vote for each state delegation, must choose a president from the three leading contestants. Clay, thus eliminated, could now play the role of kingmaker; for he not only controlled the votes of several states but wielded considerable influence as Speaker of the House. After long deliberation, Clay awarded his support to Adams. It was a logical decision, since both men favored a vigorous federal program to promote national development.

Adams, who had carried just seven states in the election, received 13 out of 24 votes in the House and thus won the presidency by a bare majority. (See the chart below.) Of the six states added to his column, three had previously voted for Clay, and three were deserters from Jackson. Jackson also lost one state to Crawford. Thus the outcome reflected distrust of Jackson, as well as the influence of Clay, among professional politicians. To the General's indignant supporters, however, it was an arrogant veto of the popular will. Then, when Adams unwisely appointed Clay as his Secretary of State, the Jacksonians set up a furious clamor, charging that their hero had been cheated by means of a "corrupt bargain." The next presidential campaign was virtually under way before Adams even took the oath of office.

The administration of John Quincy Adams exemplifies the rule that eminent statesmen do not necessarily make successful presidents. Adams had little talent for practical politics and, like most of his predecessors, only a dim understanding of the connection between political leadership and presidential power. At another time, these deficiencies might have been less critical, but the situation in 1825 called for constructive partisanship. An opposition party was taking shape and perfecting its organization. Jacksonian newspapers, growing rapidly in number, filled their columns with abuse of the administration. Calhoun had already led his followers into the Jackson camp, and soon Martin Van Buren of New York would do likewise. Both men were motivated by distrust of the Adams-Clay political philosophy and

ELECTION OF 1824			
	*States Carried**	*Electoral Votes*	*Votes in House*
Adams	7	84	13
Jackson	11	99	7
Crawford	3	41	4
Clay	3	37	—

* In five states, by a majority of the electoral votes.

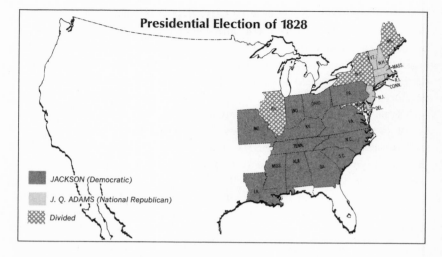

Presidential Election of 1828

JACKSON (Democratic)

J. Q. ADAMS (National Republican)

Divided

by the hope of following Old Hickory into the White House. Clay saw the need for countermeasures, and so did Daniel Webster, but their efforts to organize the friends of the administration received little help from the President. Adams would neither remove open enemies from office nor lend his prestige to political activities. Isolated by his own temperament, he remained aloof from the revolution going on all around him.

While rejecting the role of party leader, Adams aspired to be a vigorous chief executive. His first annual message was boldly Hamiltonian in spirit, recommending an extensive system of internal improvements, as well as a national university, an astronomical observatory, and a naval academy. Although such proposals were bound to antagonize the South, they should have won support for the administration in other parts of the country. But Adams fumbled his few advantages and too often gave the impression of a disdainful patrician sniffing at the common people.

Programs and issues were not very important in the bitter campaign of 1828. It was largely a personalized contest between two strikingly different men, each a target of vicious slander. For Adams, still unable to match the popular appeal of his opponent, the election results were much like those of four years earlier. He won about the same number of electoral votes in about the same states, but this time the opposition was united, well organized, and determined to avenge the "corrupt bargain." Jackson swept to an easy victory, and once again the defeat of an Adams marked a sharp turn in American political history.

THE JACKSONIANS IN POWER

The Jacksonians in 1828 were a powerful coalition of diverse elements that had no common purpose except victory. Only after coming to power did they acquire a program, an ideology, a characteristic rhetoric, and a symbolic identity. Gradually, the Democratic party emerged, although throughout Jackson's presidential tenure it continued to be essentially his personal organization.

The boisterous multitude that thronged the White House on inauguration day seemed to signify the triumph of the common people. Their hero played his part well, with just the right combination of simplicity and dignity. Yet Andrew Jackson in some ways scarcely qualified as the ideal democrat. He was a self-made man, to be sure, and his frontier background automatically endowed him with a democratic image, but he had long since become an aristocrat by Western standards. At the Hermitage, near Nashville, he ruled over a large plantation and numerous slaves in the manner of a Southern gentleman. Associated with conservative elements in Tennessee politics, he had never evinced any great urge to be a reformer or a champion of the masses. In fact, politics as a way of life did not hold much attraction for him, and his views on the major public issues were something of a mystery. Perhaps the most striking thing about Jackson was the intensely personal nature of his political conduct. He seldom forgot a friend or forgave an enemy, and private reasons can be discovered for nearly all of his important public actions.

Jackson, for example, repeatedly recommended direct popular election of the president—a democratic gesture that was also a protest against the manner of his defeat in 1825. A similar mixture of motives inspired Jackson's removal of numerous federal officeholders. He wanted to reward his supporters and punish his opponents. As a military man, he also expected unswerving loyalty from his subordinates. But at the same time he believed in the principle of rotation in office, regarding a permanent bureaucracy as undemocratic and the ordinary citizen as capable of serving his government. Actually, the spoils system neither originated nor reached its peak under Jackson. Partisan appointments began with Washington; partisan dismissals, with Jefferson. Jackson removed fewer than one-tenth of the officeholders at the beginning of his administration and about the same number during the remainder of his eight years in the presidency. Nevertheless, he set an example that was earnestly followed for the next half century. The spoils system inevitably lowered the quality of public service, but it enhanced the vitality of party politics. For the use and expectation of patronage was the lubricant that kept political machines running.

Jackson's personalism is especially apparent in his choice of advisers. Having appointed a cabinet of mediocrities, except Van Buren as Secretary of State, he seldom called it together for consultation. Instead, he relied upon an informal group of politicians and journalists that came to be known as the "Kitchen Cabinet." Two important members were Amos Kendall, who helped prepare many of Jackson's state papers, and Francis P. Blair,

The Rats leaving a Falling House.

An anti-Jackson cartoon ridiculing wholesale changes in the Cabinet during his first administration.

who became editor of the Washington *Globe* when it was established in 1830 as the administration's official organ.

Van Buren belonged to this inner circle, and so did Secretary of War John H. Eaton, one of Jackson's closest friends. When Eaton married a Washington barmaid in 1829, he set off a social controversy that had extensive political consequences. The wives of other cabinet members spurned Mrs. Eaton. Not even Jackson's warm support could gain her admission to capital society. But Van Buren, a widower, treated the Eatons with his usual graciousness and thereby entrenched himself further in the President's favor. After two years of the feud, Van Buren and Eaton resigned, giving Jackson the opportunity to reorganize his whole cabinet. Among the new appointments were Lewis Cass as Secretary of War and Roger B. Taney as Attorney General. Van Buren was named Minister to England.

One of those who suffered from the "Eaton malaria" was Calhoun. Vice-President under Adams, he had been reelected as Jackson's runningmate and hoped to succeed him. But Mrs. Calhoun, to the President's displeasure, participated in the snubbing of Mrs. Eaton. Furthermore, Calhoun was already suspected of encouraging nullification sentiment in South Carolina. By early 1830, Jackson had decided to make Van Buren his successor. He quarreled openly with Calhoun, calling him to account for having condemned the notorious Florida raid in 1818. The Vice-President's response only widened the breach beyond repair. Thus ended a struggle for power in which the Van Buren faction had all the advantages. Thereafter, Calhoun and his adherents followed a course of independent opposition to the Jackson administration.

Jackson's hostility to Calhoun soon rivaled his hatred for Clay. From a seat in the Senate, Clay was taking command of the Adams party, now known as the National Republicans. He welcomed the Vice-President's insurgency, but the two men were so far apart in their political views that they could not form a consolidated opposition. Clay was a confirmed nationalist, advocating an "American system" of protective tariffs and internal improvements as the basis for a self-sufficient economy. Calhoun had shed his earlier nationalism to become a spokesman for Southern interests and states' rights.

With enemies at both extremes, Jackson tended to occupy middle ground between Hamiltonian and Jeffersonian conceptions of the Republic. He affirmed the constitutionality of the existing tariff, for example, but favored some reduction of duties. On the subject of internal improvements he proved to be a moderate strict-constructionist. His veto of the Maysville Road bill in 1830 was directed against federal subsidization of a project that lay entirely within a single state. Yet he also signed a number of river-and-harbor appropriations that were equally local in character. Jackson was most unequivocally Jeffersonian in his opposition to the Bank of the United States, but when South Carolina directly challenged federal authority, he responded in the manner of a staunch nationalist. Both of these issues became critical in 1832. One involved him in his greatest battle with Clay; the other was a dramatic culmination of his feud with Calhoun.

NULLIFICATION

In January 1832, Calhoun enjoyed a moment of revenge when he cast the deciding vote in the Senate against confirmation of Van Buren as minister to England. Van Buren, however, returned home triumphantly to receive a higher honor. Jackson, though now in his sixty-fifth year, was preparing to run for reelection and wanted Van Buren on the ticket. Clay had already been nominated by the National Republicans, and for the first time in American history an organized third party was entering the field. A wave of resentment against the Masonic Order, originating in New York, had produced the Anti-Masonic party, with the noted Maryland lawyer, William Wirt, as its presidential candidate. It was during this campaign year that the character of Jackson's presidency became fully revealed, as he confronted the threat of nullification and the power of the Bank.

The nullification crisis developed against a background of growing Southern uneasiness about the security of slavery. To some uncertain degree, perhaps even decisively, the rise of abolitionism and the shock of Nat Turner's rebellion intensified the mood of defiance in South Carolina. A more direct and obvious influence, however, was the pressure of hard times in the South Atlantic states. Agricultural depression had settled gradually upon the tobacco regions, but for cotton planters it came as a fairly sudden reversal of postwar prosperity. South Carolina suffered the worst decline and accordingly became the center of discontent. The main problem was that the price of cotton, which had ranged as high as 30 cents a pound between 1815 and 1818, sank to 10 cents during the next decade. Although the causes of the depression were complex, Southerners tended increasingly to blame their plight upon excessive tariff rates. Protection, they maintained, reduced their foreign markets and added to the cost of their manufactured goods. The moderate tariff of 1816 had given way to a much higher schedule of duties in 1824. Four years later, as a result of some misdirected election strategy on the part of Jackson's supporters in Congress, more items were added to the protected list. Opponents called it the "tariff of abominations."

Shortly after the election of 1828, the South Carolina legislature passed a series of resolutions denouncing the tariff as both unjust and unconstitutional. Circulated with them was the *Exposition and Protest,* a document secretly drafted by Calhoun. In it the Vice-President presented the theory of nullification that he would later publicly espouse and elaborate. Drawing heavily upon the Virginia and Kentucky Resolutions, he asserted that sovereignty rested solely in the separate states, which had the ultimate power to decide whether their "agent," the federal government, had exceeded its delegated powers. Therefore, a single state could nullify any unconstitutional act of Congress, and such a decision would be binding unless overruled by an amendment to the Constitution—that is, by three-fourths of the states. Even then, the nullifying state might exercise its sovereign right to withdraw from the Union. Calhoun did not emphasize secession, however; for his purpose was by no means to destroy the Union, but rather to gain security for the South within its framework.

Several other states echoed South Carolina's protest against the tariff of 1828. But there the matter rested for a time, since Jackson's victory over Adams seemed to promise some relief from high duties. Besides, certain Southern leaders hoped to forge an alliance with the West, whereby the West would moderate its protectionism in return for support on the public lands issue. It was this strategy that drew Senator Hayne of South Carolina into his famous encounter with Webster of Massachusetts in January 1830. Webster, however, cleverly turned the debate to a discussion of nullification and emerged as an eloquent champion of national unity.

The next major tariff law was passed in 1832. A number of duties were reduced, but chiefly those on noncompetitive items, while the measure clearly retained the principle of protection. As a step in the right direction, it received considerable Southern support and Jackson's signature. In South Carolina, however, there was not only bitter disappointment but bold action. The legislature called a state convention, which met in November and promptly adopted an ordinance nullifying the tariffs of 1828 and 1832. Collection of duties within South Carolina was prohibited, beginning February 1, and the ordinance further declared that a resort to force by the federal government would justify secession. Grimly, the state legislature authorized the raising of a military force.

Jackson met the crisis with a proclamation to the people of South Carolina in which he emphatically refuted the doctrine of nullification, promised to execute the law by force if necessary, and denounced armed secession as treason. At his request, Congress prepared to enact a Force bill giving him additional coercive powers. Meanwhile, South Carolina found itself standing alone, as the other Southern states refused to support nullification. Jackson, however, had mixed firmness with conciliation by recommending a reduction of duties. Facing overwhelming odds, the South Carolinians, in an irregular convention, suspended the operation of their nullifying ordinance, pending the outcome of tariff legislation. At this point, Henry Clay the nationalist became Clay the compromiser again. He introduced a bill providing for the gradual reduction of duties over a ten-year period. It passed Congress on March 1, 1833, along with the Force Bill, and Jackson signed both measures the following day. With the approval of Calhoun, who had resigned as Vice-President and had accepted election to the Senate, a new South Carolina convention rescinded the ordinance of nullification. In a last gesture of defiance, it also nullified the Force Act, but the latter, of course, was no longer needed. The crisis had passed.

Both sides claimed victory, and with good reason, but nullification had clearly been something less than a success. In its place, secession received increasing consideration as the ultimate means of protecting Southern rights. Furthermore, the experience of South Carolina had shown that a single state could not act very effectively without strong sectional support. The nullification crisis thus contributed to the growth of Southern nationalism.

THE BANK WAR

The Bank of the United States was not primarily a sectional issue, although it could count upon more support from the Northeast than from other parts of the country. Neither was the Bank any longer a critical constitutional issue, despite Jacksonian efforts to make it so, for that question had been settled by usage and by the Supreme Court. Nor did the struggle over the Bank pit one class against another; the institution had staunch friends and bitter enemies within the business community, for example. Finally, not even Jackson succeeded in making the Bank a clear-cut partisan issue, for a sizable minority of Democrats disagreed with him on the subject.

Opposition to the Bank came from a curious combination of interests. One element was generally hostile to all banks and to the paper money system. It included many farmers and workingmen who preferred to be paid in specie, as well as men like Jackson himself whose personal experience

The Bank War, with Andrew Jackson squaring off against Nicholas Biddle. The other figures, left to right, are "Old Mother Bank," Daniel Webster, Henry Clay, Martin Van Buren, Jack Downing, and a Tammany warrior.

and observation had produced a sour attitude toward banking. On the other hand, there were debtor and entrepreneurial elements that resented the Bank's regulatory activities. They wanted freer banking, easier credit, and more money in circulation. In spite of these different purposes, however, all such groups could agree that the Bank wielded too much economic power, too much political influence, and was therefore a threat to republican government. Jackson, characteristically, came to view the matter as a personal combat between him and the monster of Chestnut Street. "The Bank is trying to kill me, but I will kill it," he supposedly declared.

The Bank's 20-year charter did not expire until 1836, but Nicholas Biddle, its president, was understandably worried by Jackson's openly hostile attitude. At Clay's urging, Biddle decided to press for renewal of the charter in 1832. Jackson, they hoped, either would not dare offer opposition in an election year or would be repudiated at the polls if he did. A bill to recharter the

Bank passed both houses of Congress by comfortable margins, but the President vetoed it on July 10. He justified his action in a strongly worded message depicting the institution as a monopoly unconstitutionally vested with special privileges. Efforts to override the veto ended in failure, and the Bank became the principal issue of the presidential campaign. On election day, Jackson won a decisive victory over Clay (219 electoral votes to 47), with Wirt, the Anti-Masonic candidate, carrying only Vermont.

With a majority of Americans apparently on his side, Jackson determined to strike another blow at the Bank by withdrawing the government funds that it held on deposit. Two successive Secretaries of the Treasury refused to do his bidding, and not until the appointment of Taney in September 1833 did the strategy succeed. The government began to deposit its funds in a selected group of state banks, derisively labeled Jackson's "pets." Resolutions censuring the President for his action were introduced in the Senate by Clay and were approved. Jackson responded with a "protest" eloquently defending the independence of the chief executive, who, he said, was the only direct representative of the people as a whole.

Meanwhile, Biddle had initiated a program of tighter credit, partly in order to strengthen his own financial position, partly to bring pressure on

The Second Bank of the United States in Philadelphia—Biddle's "Monster" and also an excellent example of Greek Revival architecture.

Congress. But the resulting distress only made the Bank more unpopular and killed any lingering hope for a new charter. In 1836, it became a state bank, incorporated by Pennsylvania. For the hard-money Jacksonians, however, the consequences of victory proved disillusioning. Federal money deposited in the "pet banks" enabled them to increase their loans, while other state banks, no longer feeling Biddle's restraining hand, likewise expanded their credit and note issues. The resulting inflation encouraged reckless speculation, especially in Western lands. Jackson tried to apply a brake with his "Specie Circular" of July 11, 1836, which announced that only gold or silver would be accepted in payment for public land. The sudden deflationary effect of this action helped bring on the Panic of 1837.

DEMOCRATS AND WHIGS

By 1834, the various opponents of the administration had begun to coalesce, adopting the name "Whig" as a symbol of middle-class liberalism and resistance to executive tyranny. National Republicans were joined by Anti-Masons, disgruntled Southerners, and rebellious Democrats. Jackson's war on the Bank drove about 28 Democratic congressmen into the Whig ranks. Although the new party drew support from all sections and classes, it tended to be socially conservative, somewhat patrician in tone, and closely linked with urban business interests. Many of the wealthiest Southern planters became Whigs, and in the North, the party was generally favored by people of New England Puritan stock. On the other hand, it failed to attract Germans and Irish, the two largest immigrant groups, or to win over a majority of Western farmers. Yet Whiggery had a progressive as well as a conservative side. Its membership included men of constructive outlook and social conscience whose faith in the potential of a democratic society equaled that of the Jacksonians.

When the campaign of 1836 began, however, the Whig party was still being formed. The Democrats nominated Van Buren, as expected, while the Whigs chose to support several candidates, each appealing to a different section of the country. Van Buren emerged the victor over four opponents, but received only a bare majority of the popular vote. One surprising result was the strong showing made by William Henry Harrison, who ran far ahead of the other Whig candidates and thus established himself as a leading contender for the nomination in 1840.

Fortune ceased to smile on Van Buren when he entered the White House. The Panic of 1837 was already under way, and economic distress persisted to the end of his term. Placing much of the blame on the banking system, he recommended that the federal government divorce itself from all banks by acting as its own fiscal agent. In 1840, after three years of Whig resistance, Congress created the Independent Treasury. Van Buren's administration was also troubled by difficulties with England, growing out of an abortive revolution in Canada and a boundary dispute between Maine and New Brunswick. In both cases, the President acted swiftly and wisely to preserve peace, but he angered many Americans who favored a more belligerent policy. At the same time, abolitionist agitation and Southern responses to it were producing bitter discord in Congress. Especially provocative was the problem of handling the growing number of antislavery petitions. A House resolution, approved in 1836, ordered that all such documents be tabled without printing or reference to a committee. The fight in each session against this "gag rule" was led by John Quincy Adams, now a representative from Massachusetts, but not until 1844 did he succeed in having it rescinded.

The Democrats consequently entered the campaign of 1840 on the defensive, renominating Van Buren without much enthusiasm. Scenting victory, the Whigs passed over Clay and named Harrison as their candidate. They added John Tyler of Virginia to the ticket in a bid for Southern votes. Now it was the Whigs' turn to exploit the frontier theme and to hurrah for their own military hero, who had defeated the Indians at Tippecanoe and turned back the British in the War of 1812. They portrayed Harrison as an honest, plain-spoken man of the people, and Van Buren as a ridiculous, luxury-loving dandy. Never before had a party plunged into a contest with such exuberant energy or promoted its candidate with so much oratory and pageantry, so many slogans and stunts and popular demonstrations. The Whigs, in this "log cabin and hard cider" campaign of 1840, completely outplayed the Democrats at their own game. "We have taught them to conquer us," lamented the *Democratic Review* in June. It was an accurate prediction; for Harrison won 234 electoral votes to Van Buren's 60, and the Whigs also captured control of Congress.

Harrison appointed a strong cabinet headed by Webster as Secretary of State, while Clay prepared to direct Whig strategy from his seat in the Senate. But then, after just one month in office, the 68-year-old President died of pneumonia, to be succeeded by a states'-rights Democrat who had changed parties because of his hostility to Jackson. John Tyler, despite arguments

A Whig cartoon in the campaign of 1840. Harrison topples Van Buren and his underlings, Francis P. Blair and Amos Kendall.

to the contrary, insisted that he was now president in every sense of the word. He thus set a precedent that has been followed ever since. Tyler also made it plain that he would not submit to Clay's dictation. Twice "His Accidency" vetoed bills for the reestablishment of a national bank, and on the second occasion, all members of the cabinet except Webster resigned in protest. Certain other Whig measures received Tyler's approval, including the Distribution-Preemption bill, an increase in tariff rates to the level of 1832, and repeal of the Independent Treasury Act. Yet he had clearly become an isolated figure, a president repudiated by his own party, and leadership of the Whigs was once more in Clay's firm grasp.

Although bad luck had partially nullified their victory, the Whigs were now firmly established as the second party in a functioning two-party system. Yet this apparently stable alignment would last for only three more presidential elections. The two potentially disruptive factors were the persistence of the slavery controversy and the rising tide of immigration, which was already producing a nativist reaction. The Liberty party, organized by abolitionists, polled only a few thousand votes in 1840, but like a small, dark cloud on the horizon, it carried the threat of an approaching storm. New York nativists formed the American Republican party in 1843. Efforts at national organization were unsuccessful, but they had broken a trail for the Know Nothings of the 1850s. Nativism eventually played havoc with Whig unity, while the slavery issue was destined to split both major parties before it disrupted the Union itself.

THE JACKSONIAN TRADITION

"Jacksonian" is an adjective of many uses, and its meaning varies with the context. The word may refer to the personal historical role of Andrew Jackson himself or to the political party built around him. It also designates a fairly definite era in history, together with the dominant ideas, values, and aspirations of that era. In a sense, there was only one veritable Jacksonian, and yet all Americans of the time were in some degree Jacksonians.

Jackson, it is clear, reversed a drift toward executive weakness and thus exerted profound influence upon the presidency as an institution. He used the veto more extensively than any of his predecessors, and in the Bank struggle he firmly asserted his independence of Congress and the Supreme Court, as well as his authority over the cabinet. Jackson's personal forcefulness was doubly effective because of his strong partisan position. Even more than Jefferson, he merged the roles of chief executive and party leader, strengthening both in the process. Yet, at the same time, Jackson projected the image of the president as tribune of the whole people, responsible only to them for his actions.

As the first Westerner in the White House and the first military man since Washington, Jackson brought a new style to the presidency and became one of the great symbolic figures in American politics. Breaking the tradition of scholar-statesmen, he represented the virile genius of the frontier, the man of action whose natural wisdom was unspoiled by the artificialities of book learning. This anti-intellectualism in the Jacksonian image reflected the leveling tendencies of the democratic faith. It also exemplified a nationalistic urge to be free of "effete" European influences. But in addition, the legendary Jackson—one of nature's noblemen, relying upon intuition and will rather than refined intellect—was a literary creation worthy of the romantic era.

Jackson's assertion of executive authority was in the Hamiltonian tradition, but otherwise the Democratic party tended to embrace the "negative liberalism" of Jefferson. The Jacksonians, to be sure, were far from presenting a united front on major public issues, and political theory seldom played an important part in the shaping of their attitudes and decisions. Nevertheless, the aggregate of Democratic policies amounted to a moderate reaction against the drift toward centralization and economic nationalism in the decade following the War of 1812.

This tendency was reflected in decisions of the Supreme Court, especially after Roger B. Taney succeeded John Marshall as Chief Justice in 1836. A Maryland Catholic and slaveholder, Taney had been Jackson's right-hand man during the Bank war, and in the Whig view, his appointment was a calamity. No revolution in constitutional law ensued, but the Taney Court did substantially modify the structure of interpretation built up under Marshall. In general, its decisions allowed more latitude to state governments and placed somewhat less emphasis upon property rights and national supremacy.

Two cases decided in 1837 show the Jacksonian temper of the Taney Court. In *Briscoe v. The Bank of Kentucky,* the justices upheld the legality of bank notes issued by a state-owned bank. This decision conflicted sharply with an earlier Marshall opinion on the subject and ignored the plain intention of the men who framed the Constitution. Yet, as a corollary to the overthrow of Biddle's "monster," it was definitely in tune with the times. In *Charles River Bridge v. Warren Bridge,* the Court denied that monopoly rights could be implied from a corporate charter. Any such charter grant, Taney declared, must be strictly construed, with ambiguities always resolved in favor of state authority. Here was an important limitation placed upon Marshall's Dartmouth College doctrine, although it by no means destroyed the effectiveness of the contract clause as a protection of business enterprise against arbitrary government. The Court also took a relatively broad view of state police power in several decisions concerning interstate commerce. Except on the subject of slavery, Taney and his associates tended to be moderate champions of majority rule and democratic social control.

In its broadest sense, however, the phrase "Jacksonian Democracy" is a label pinned to a generation—useful for identification but somewhat misleading as a description of the historical forces at work. The process of liberalizing the suffrage and otherwise democratizing the political system neither began nor ended with Andrew Jackson. If his age did exhibit revolutionary characteristics, they had more to do with the content of democracy than with its external forms.

The principle of popular sovereignty had flowered during the Revolution, and its roots extended back into the colonial era. Jefferson, in the Declaration of Independence, had posited the equality of men in order to justify self-government; and self-government, in turn, was the indispensable means of protecting individual liberties. Thus Jefferson argued from equality to liberty, and quite understandably so in 1776, when his assigned task was the vindication of resistance to British "tyranny." But by Jackson's time, circumstances were tending to produce an inversion of the argument. Liberty, no longer threatened after 1815, became a cherished possession rather than an object of aspiration. The paramount question now was what a free man could make of himself. From his birthright of freedom, the Jacksonian American inferred a claim to equality—not of condition but of opportunity. The quickening tempo of westward expansion and economic change was multiplying the outlets for impatient ambition, and it is not surprising that in such a setting, opportunity should have been defined largely in materialistic terms. As a consequence, contemporary observers like Tocqueville often arrived at the not entirely accurate conclusion that Americans valued liberty less than equality and material well-being.

The egalitarian spirit was often expressed in negative ways. Jacksonian Americans knew what they opposed better than what they wanted. The crux of the matter was their hostility to aristocratic pretension and entrenched privilege. Property qualifications for voting and the Bank of the United States were alike in representing advantages unfairly extended to some men and withheld from others. Southerners protested that the protective tariff unjustly favored industry at the expense of agriculture. Northern attacks on slavery were aimed in part at the privileged position of the institution under the three-fifths compromise, as well as the stratified social order that it perpetuated. The spoils system was a democratic thrust against privileged bureaucracy. Egalitarian impulses did not originate in any one section, but the symbols of equality were taken primarily from the Western scene, where opportunity seemed most abundant and aristocracy most ridiculous. This symbolic power of the frontier, so well exemplified in the election of 1840, tends to obscure the fact that throughout the entire country, the Jacksonian era was a time when the word "democracy" was acquiring new meanings to express the expanding aspirations of the people.

Chapter VI

The Varieties of American Experience

THE AMERICAN MULTITUDE

An Englishwoman traveling by steamboat from New Orleans to Cincinnati in 1828 took note of the woodcutters who supplied fuel to the passing vessels. The wretchedness apparent in their crude shanties (usually inundated in high water) was also plainly written on their faces. "These unhappy beings," she observed, "are invariably the victims of ague, which they meet recklessly, sustained by the incessant use of ardent spirits. The squalid look of the miserable wives and children of these men was dreadful. . . . Their complexion is of a blueish white, that suggests the idea of dropsy; this is invariable, and the poor little ones wear exactly the same ghastly hue. A miserable cow and a few pigs, standing knee-deep in water, distinguish the more prosperous of these dwellings; and on the whole I should say that I never witnessed human nature reduced so low as it appeared in the woodcutters' huts on the unwholesome banks of the Mississippi."

The woodcutter played a humble but essential role in a major historical event—the rise of steamboat travel during the early nineteenth century. Otherwise, there were but slender and intermittent connections between the life that he lived and what passes for the history of his times. The unique rhythms of his miserable existence are below the level of historical notice. He belongs, in fact, to the nonhistorical multitude, whose nameless members are treated only as types and are sometimes scooped up in broad generalizations about the "American people." Written history provides at best a meager remnant of the past; for no language can convey the rich variety and infinite complexity of human experience.

National history usually stresses the formally organized behavior of a people acting together as a nation (especially the politics, diplomacy, and wars of their central government), along with other events and experiences, that significantly affect either national public policy or a large part of the national population. Much harder to distil into historical narrative are those experiences which are not shared widely throughout a nation, those events of great local but slight national importance, those patterns of repetitive behavior that change slowly and undramatically but make up a large part of the average man's life. At the personal level in early nineteenth-century America, a state law, a local flood, a new medical remedy, or the eloquence of a now forgotten preacher could have far more meaning than the contemporary events that were destined to be recorded in history books. The discrepancy between history and life is inevitable because of life's incomprehensible variety, but it should at least be duly acknowledged whenever the past is reduced to print.

Alexis de Tocqueville, that perceptive interpreter of American democracy in the 1830s, saw disturbing signs of a trend toward mass conformity. Individualism could be stifled, he thought, by equalitarian pressures and the enormous power of public opinion in the United States. A new kind of despotism would then emerge, resting squarely upon the principle of majority rule and suppressing personal liberty by intellectual and emotional force, rather than by physical compulsion. It was a warning that gathered additional meaning with the passing years, and yet the worst has never happened. More than a century later, another friendly critic from abroad provided an interesting sequel to Tocqueville's misgivings. "Americanism," wrote Harold J. Laski, "is multiform, and it is also, at its very roots, nonconformist. No one can fully shape it the way he wants it to go—no president and no millionaire, no labour leader and no intellectual; and it is not even shaped by all the objective consequences of its mass production system. Something is always escaping to be itself. . ."

Tocqueville's judgment was strongly influenced, of course, by his knowledge of European society. Americans of the Jacksonian era were indeed more alike than Frenchmen in many ways. Regional differences were far less deeply rooted, for example, and social classes were neither as widely nor as clearly and firmly separated. Still, close scrutiny of American patterns of culture in the early nineteenth century reveals a diversity that is especially bewildering because the variations were not only often subtle and informal, but usually in flux. And from the American multitude, despite all the factors promoting homogeneity, something was perpetually escaping to be itself.

OLD AMERICANS AND NEW

Although predominantly English in its population and culture, the American nation of 1800 already contained many ethnic minorities. There were the descendants of the Scotch-Irish and Germans who had swarmed across the Atlantic during the eighteenth century, as well as smaller numbers of Dutch, Scots, French Huguenots, Jews, and other peoples. In addition, the population of 5.3 million included 1 million Negroes, nine-tenths of them slaves.

Some of these non-English elements clung tenaciously to their own cultural traditions—notably the Pennsylvania Germans in communities like Lancaster and Reading. On the whole, however, the period from the Revolution to 1815 was one of rapid Americanization. Dutch and German declined as public languages, for example. English replaced them in many church services, and the number of foreign-language newspapers decreased. The Negro, of course, had been swiftly and forcibly detached from his African heritage without being fully integrated into American society. Slavery fixed him in a special, inferior status, separate from the rest of the population in some respects and yet closely associated with it in others. Free Negroes, already subject to many legal disabilities, were in a more anomalous position, but they lacked the numbers, solidarity, and influence to do anything but accept their lot.

Americanization was facilitated by the relatively light influx of immigrants from Europe, amounting to about 300,000 during the first forty years of independence. The reluctance of many countries to permit emigration, together with the wars that occupied much of the period, greatly restricted the movement of people across the Atlantic. Importation of slaves continued under constitutional protection until 1808, when Congress made it illegal, but the Negro's servile place was waiting for him upon arrival. Thus, during the critical early years of the Republic, the consolidation of nationality proceeded without the distraction of having to assimilate large numbers of strangers. Less than 5 percent of the population growth in the first three decades of the nineteenth century resulted from immigration.

The change began in the 1820s and gathered momentum thereafter until mass immigration reached a peak of three million during the decade of 1845 to 1854. This influx, although later exceeded numerically, was the largest in proportion to the total population that the nation ever experienced. It had an incalculable effect upon virtually every aspect of American culture, including economic growth, social institutions, party politics, and religion.

The three major countries of origin, in their order of numerical importance, were Ireland, Germany, and Great Britain. Together, they supplied
about 85 percent of all the immigrants entering the United States between
1820 and 1860. Among the factors that encouraged the coming of so
many people were the removal of barriers against emigration, the development
of relatively cheap ocean transportation, a growing awareness of opportunities
in America, and troubles at home like the great Irish potato famine of the
late 1840s.

British immigrants tended to disperse widely and blend readily with the
native-born population. Their collective influence is therefore extremely
difficult to measure. The Irish, on the other hand, concentrated heavily in
the urban centers of the Northeast, and those who did go west also headed
for the cities. Generally not only poor but without education and occupa-
tional skill, they could seldom obtain work other than as common laborers
or servants. Some of them found higher-paying, backbreaking jobs on
construction gangs, and by the 1840s, others were moving into industrial
employment, but as a whole, the Irish continued to be near the bottom
of the economic scale. As for the Germans, although some had the capital
and skill to become farmers, the majority of them also concentrated in
Northern cities. They spread out more than the Irish, however, especially
along the lakes and rivers of the Old Northwest, and they entered a wider
variety of occupations. Separated by language from the rest of the population, German immigrants achieved greater solidarity in America than they
had ever experienced in their homeland, and they made strenuous efforts
to preserve and transplant the old, familiar ways of life.

Statistical tables greatly understate the remarkable variety added by
immigration to the ethnic fabric of the nation; for within each general
grouping there were numerous cultural strains. Native Americans often failed
to understand how different Prussians were from Bavarians, Ulstermen from
Dubliners, and Welshmen from Cockneys. What caught their attention
instead were the ways in which immigrants deviated from American norms.
Here, a matter of primary importance was religious affiliation. Just as the
Scotch-Irish had once expanded the influence of Presbyterianism, so Germans
and Scandinavians now made Lutheranism a major denomination in the
United States. But since many Germans and most of the Irish were Catholics,
it was the Church of Rome that gained the most ground as a result of
mass immigration.

Immigration was usually a physical and psychological ordeal for the immigrant, who found himself suddenly detached from the world of his own experience, socially isolated in a strange and sometimes hostile environment. At the same time, the growing volume of new arrivals could not fail to have a profoundly disturbing effect upon many native Americans. The result in the first case was a sense of alienation and helplessness amounting frequently to trauma; the result in the second case was a cluster of attitudes and actions collectively labeled "nativism."

By no means an entirely new element in American history, nativism ranged from mild suspicion of foreigners to virulent bigotry and hatred, from concealed thought to violent action, and from the accurate perception of real evils to pathological fears of approaching disaster. It reflected selfish personal considerations and patriotic concern for the future of the nation. The object of its resentment might be the whole, or only a certain part, of the immigrant population. In general, however, nativists were people who tended to see nothing but danger in cultural pluralism and to equate national strength with national homogeneity. The unfortunate consequence was a pattern of reciprocal distrust. When ethnic groups found a measure of security by drawing together in their own communities, they seemed all the more clannish and unassimilable.

Immigrants supplied the cheap labor needed for economic expansion and thus aroused the animosity of native workers by competing for their jobs and depressing wages. In time, this rivalry became fiercer, but American labor before the Civil War was not yet strong enough to mobilize an effective anti-immigration campaign. More pressing were the urban social problems resulting from the immigrant's poverty, especially disease, crime, pauperism, and the proliferation of slums. The disproportionately large numbers of foreigners crowding city jails and lengthening relief rolls convinced many Americans that immigrants, particularly Irish immigrants, were incorrigibly depraved and vicious. Too few considered the possibility that such widespread misery and degradation might be evidence of social injustice, rather than ethnic character. Even the happier aspects of immigrant life could stir up controversy. The European's Sunday, for example, violated sober Puritan tradition. Germans were the most conspicuous offenders, as they hurried from church to a merry afternoon in music halls and beer gardens. Heavy drinking and public drunkenness, all too common in immigrant communities, likewise became standard objects of censure. Sabbatarian and prohibition crusades were both directed, to a considerable degree, against the foreign-born elements in the population.

A more intense feeling was aroused by the spectacular expansion of Catholicism. A "Protestant crusade" took shape during the 1820s and grew in proportion to immigration. It sprang from secular as well as religious sources, reflecting not only a traditional abhorrence of "Popery" but also a strong conviction that the authoritarian character of the Catholic Church made it incompatible with American principles and institutions. One center of conflict was the school system in New York, where Catholic leaders set off a bitter controversy by demanding a share of state educational funds and denouncing the use of the Protestant Bible in public schools. There were also outbreaks of mob violence, such as the burning of the Ursuline Convent near Boston in 1834 and the riots that shook Philadelphia ten years later. But for the most part, the crusade was a propaganda war, marked by a vast outpouring of vehement and often scurrilous anti-Catholic literature. Many foreign-born Protestants joined in these assaults, even while suffering themselves from the abuse directed at all immigrants. Thus anti-Catholicism, though closely related to nativism, was not synonymous with it. The Catholic Church, in any case, continued to flourish, and its adherents retained liberties far exceeding those conceded to Protestants in the Catholic countries of the world.

Still another evil effect attributed to immigration was the corruption of the American political process. The Irish, especially, were accused of voting illegally, of selling their votes to unscrupulous politicians, and of causing disturbances at the polls. Each of these charges could be supported with considerable evidence. Yet the more fundamental problem was that immigrants tended to vote as blocs, and in many communities they held the balance of political power. Their general preference for the Democratic parties of Jefferson and Jackson stimulated nativist sentiment among the opposition, from the Federalists to the Whigs. Eventually, the growing influence of foreign-born voters inspired the battle-cry: "Americans shall rule America."

Nativism, originating as a social protest against immigrant influence, was rather slow in becoming a significant political movement. Although the Alien and Sedition Acts of the 1790s may be regarded as an early manifestation, political nativism did not really make its appearance until about 1840. Then Native American organizations began to spring up locally in all parts of the country. Most successful was the American Republican party of New York, organized in 1843 and strong enough to carry the New York City election a year later. At a convention held in Philadelphia on July 4, 1845, the party proclaimed itself national in scope. These nativists made no effort to secure restriction of immigration itself. Instead, they demanded a lengthening of the naturalization period to 21 years, as well as the exclusion of immigrants from officeholding. Their main purpose was to destroy the foreigner's political power. Nativism suffered some decline in the later 1840s, when the nation became preoccupied with territorial expansion and the slavery controversy. But it quickly revived and flourished as the Know Nothing movement of the 1850s.

INSTITUTIONAL MOLDS

Men are ordinarily known to history by the social roles they have played. The American of the early nineteenth-century, sturdy individualist though he might be in many respects, was also a roleplayer. Like men of other ages, he spent much of his life following routines established by the social groups and institutions with which he was associated. At this particular time, however, the structure of American society was subject to abnormal pressures that produced not only bewildering change but a distinctive set of contradictory tendencies.

For one thing, traditional institutions were losing much of their earlier authority because of the disruptive influence of westward expansion, mass immigration, and social mobility. People on the move inevitably cut some of their old cultural ties. Class lines were dissolving; organized religion was becoming increasingly fragmented; political leadership, once a matter of negotiation within a small elite, now depended upon popularity among the masses. The general dispersal of power, exemplified in the downfall of Biddle's Bank, weakened institutional control of social behavior. And yet the same forces promoted certain counter-tendencies. The free individual in a mass society could accomplish little by himself. A man entering a new environment or wrestling with a new problem soon found that he needed help. His solution, very often, was to form some kind of organization, dedicated to a specific purpose. Voluntary associations, seemingly infinite in number and variety, filled part of the void created by the decline of institutional authority. "The Americans," Tocqueville observed, "make associations to give entertainments, to found seminaries, to build inns, to construct churches, to diffuse books, to send missionaries to the antipodes; in this manner they found hospitals, prisons, and schools. If it is proposed to inculcate some truth or to foster some feeling by the encouragement

A mid-century fire engine used in Morrisania, New York.

of a great example, they form a society." These proliferating private organizations were vehicles of cooperative effort, but they did not restore the organic coherence of eighteenth-century society.

Voluntary associations illustrate the trend toward specialization in an emerging urban-industrial order. The roles to be played were becoming more numerous and specific. Yet, as a counter-tendency especially characteristic of the Jacksonian era, one must note the readiness and ease with which Americans shifted from one role to another. For instance, the professions of law and medicine required so little formal training that a man might try both, with perhaps some teaching, farming, and banking along the way. And of course it was part of the Jacksonian creed that any intelligent citizen was capable of holding public office. Samuel F. B. Morse won fame as a painter and notoriety as a leader propagandist in the anti-Catholic crusade before joining the ranks of major inventors. Such versatility was common, but few men had the talents to equal their roving ambitions, and the result too often was mediocrity instead of excellence. The day of the expert had not yet arrived.

The American family remained more stable than most institutions during the first half of the nineteenth century, and its significance as the primary social unit is therefore sometimes overlooked. Family ties linked the plantation elites of the South and high society in Northern cities; they formed webs of power in business and politics; they helped shape the patterns of immigration and internal migration. One could make a long list of public men—like John Tyler, John C. Fremont, and Stephen A. Douglas—whose marriages profoundly influenced their careers. The mobility of the population tended to disperse families, but to broaden the scope of family connections. During the 1850s, for example, four brothers named Washburn were among the founders of the Republican party in four different states from Maine to California. Three of them served in Congress together, and the fourth was a leading journalist in his state.

In a predominantly rural society, the family continued to be the basic economic unit—for production as well as for consumption. Children were generally an economic asset, and the birth rate, although declining steadily with the advance of urbanization, was still relatively high in 1850. The home functioned then, more than it does today, as a center of practical education and religious instruction. It was also the center of tragic experience. Sickness and early death were common, and a high mortality rate among children in particular cast dark shadows over family life.

Inherently a conservative institution, the family yielded but slowly to the equalitarian influences of the age. The confirmed democrat abroad was still, by law and ancient custom, a monarch at home. There, wife and children were subject to his will and had few rights of their own. If discipline required it, he could beat them, one and all, without interference. A married woman's position was virtually that of a perpetual minor. Her husband controlled even the property that she brought to the marriage; he could appropriate her earnings; and his decisions were final in matters such as the education of their children. In practice, to be sure, mutual affection and respect often moderated the severity of legal tradition. Many a wife, far from being an abjectly subservient creature, was the real ruler of her household. Women set the standards of polite society, and in the pioneering West, where they were badly needed and scarce in relation to the number of men, their status tended to be high.

Furthermore, the family could not remain immune to social change. As more and more children attended school or worked in factories, the home had to compete with other influences. The decline of parental authority became a common complaint. For women, industrial employment was a step toward independence. By mid-century, with coeducation now advancing to the college level, women were also teaching school in large numbers. A few had even invaded professions like law and medicine. Female property rights were being liberalized in some states, and although the demand for woman suffrage met with general ridicule, the issue had at least been placed before the public. It was still a man's world, but somewhat less so than in 1800.

A much less stable institution than the family during this period was the church, which seemed to be in a state of perpetual revolution. Some of the profoundest changes were but a continuation of religious trends dating back to the colonial era; others resulted from new social influences arising in the nineteenth century.

The United States in 1800 was overwhelmingly a Protestant nation, with some degree of religious unity. Despite certain differences, the major churches—Congregational, Presbyterian, Baptist, and Episcopal (Anglican)— were within the Calvinist tradition. What is more, these Protestant bodies tended to be denominational, rather than sectarian; that is, they acknowledged that other organizations besides their own were legitimate followers of Christ. The rise of Catholicism, while providing an additional reason for Protestant solidarity, had a divisive effect upon the population as a whole, since the exclusive claims of the Catholic Church amounted to uncompromising sectarianism in the American setting. Catholicism, indeed, was self-sufficient and separate from the mainstream of American history. Protestantism remained the dominant mode and reflected the significant religious trends of the time.

The separation of religion from government, already achieved at the national level and in all but three states by 1800, meant that the various Protestant churches were voluntary associations. They competed for members among themselves, but also acted as allies against religious indifference. The work of spreading the gospel was carried on not only by the churches themselves but through the affiliated activities of Sunday schools, tract societies, and missionary organizations. The most dramatic means of recruitment, however, were the recurring efforts at mass conversion known as religious revivals. Although evangelism had originated in the colonial period, its strong emotional appeal suited the temper of the early nineteenth century and proved especially effective on the moving frontier. Consequently, while all Protestant denominations felt the influence of revivalism, those using its techniques with the greatest ardor and skill enjoyed the most rapid growth. By the 1830s, the Methodist and Baptist churches had become the two largest in the country.

The rise of Methodism may be the best indicator of what was happening to American Protestantism as a whole. This denomination flourished because of its vigorous revivalism and because its organizational methods, like the circuit-rider system, were well adapted to the needs of an expanding nation. But Methodism also offered a comforting theology that was part of a general reaction against the Calvinist view of God and man. The stern Puritan doctrines of total depravity, predestination, and selective salvation were in conflict with the democratic and optimistic spirit of the age. One revolt within the Congregational Church produced Unitarianism, a rationalistic modification that suited New England intellectuals but failed to win widespread support. More popular was the Methodist belief in free will and salvation through a highly personal experience of repentance and conversion, with an accompanying reduction of emphasis on theological doctrine. These tendencies affected even the traditional Calvinist churches, and there is

A lithographer's impression of a religious camp meeting.

considerable truth in the assertion that by mid-century, Puritanism had given way to Methodism as the representative expression of the Protestant faith in America.

Religious change during the early nineteenth century mirrored many of the trends in secular society, for it bore the marks of democracy, individualism, competitive enterprise, and romantic faith in the perfectability of man. As an institutional structure, religion also exemplified the general social drift toward fragmentation and dispersal of authority. Proliferation of churches and sects, a tendency inherent in Protestantism, was further encouraged by the American environment of freedom and restless mobility. Many of these groups, including the Lutherans and German Pietists, had been transplanted earlier from Europe. Others, such as the Unitarians and Disciples of Christ, were born of secession from existing churches. Still others, like the Latter-Day Saints (Mormons) and Millerites (Adventists), sprang up as indigenous originals. At the same time, internal dissension troubled most denominations and in some cases produced outright schisms. Doctrinal and organizational controversies were uppermost at first, but soon the slavery issue became the greatest strain on ecclesiastical unity. When both the Baptist and Methodist churches split apart along sectional lines in 1844 and 1845, they provided an ominous preview of what lay ahead for the nation.

While religion was formally separating from government, American education moved in the opposite direction. Except in New England, colonial education had been left largely to the churches and private initiative, with parents usually paying the cost. Poor children were sometimes accepted as charity cases, but more often their only opportunity was apprenticeship in a trade. Even the tax-supported common schools of New England collected tuition from those who could afford it, and the quality of education in many localities fell far below the standards set by law. The nation's great stake in educational progress, emphatically affirmed by Revolutionary leaders like John Adams and Thomas Jefferson, became more obvious with the advance of political democracy. "In a republic," Horace Mann declared, "ignorance is a crime." Yet the movement for free public schools met strong resistance. It had to overcome the inertia of tradition, the property owner's fear of increased taxes, and church opposition to secularized education. Furthermore, the principle was always much easier to proclaim than to put into practice. Laws providing for public education sometimes continued for years to be little more than statements of purpose.

The disposition to regard free education as charity died hard, especially in the South where private schools and tutors served the upper classes. Not until after the Civil War did most Southern states establish effective public-school systems. Elsewhere, state laws often left the final decision to local option with varying results. Moreover, even when public education for all children won acceptance, the schools usually did not receive full tax support. Until 1867, New York continued a policy of charging "rate bills" to parents when public funds were exhausted. Yet by mid-century it was already abundantly clear that the advocates of free public schools were winning their long battle.

Another aspect of the struggle was the continuing effort to improve the quality of schools already established. Horace Mann, secretary of the Massachusetts State Board of Education from 1837 to 1848, introduced professional training for teachers and raised their salaries, lengthened the school year to six months, encouraged revision of the curriculum, and aroused public support for the provision of better schoolhouses and teaching materials. In many other states, similar leaders pursued the same objectives, though seldom with as much success.

Nonpublic elementary schools by no means disappeared; indeed, they multiplied rapidly after 1850 as the Catholic Church developed its parochial system. Meanwhile, secondary education was carried on largely in private academies, which had replaced the colonial Latin schools and probably numbered more than 6000 on the eve of the Civil War. On the other hand, a spectacular expansion of higher education resulted from combined public and private efforts. As the population moved westward, denominational colleges sprang up by the score, attesting to the vigor and competitiveness of American churches. More of an innovation was the state university, which appeared first in Pennsylvania and North Carolina, but became identified especially with the West, where private resources were generally unavailable for such ambitious educational ventures. At the same time, a growing realization that education should extend beyond childhood inspired the rise of the Lyceum movement during the Jacksonian period; and soon permanent institutes were offering instruction to workingmen in several of the major cities. Thus, in a variety of ways, education was becoming an American birthright.

THE DISCOVERY OF SOCIAL EVIL

The American people, Tocqueville remarked in 1831, were so accustomed to change that they had come to regard it as the "natural state of man." More than that, they appeared to have an unlimited faith in human perfectability. "There is not a country in the world," he wrote, "where man more confidently seizes the future, where he so proudly feels that his intelligence makes him master of the universe, that he can fashion it to his liking." And such thoughts were expressed not only by the intellectual, but by the farmer and artisan. "They inhere in all objects," exclaimed the young Frenchman. "They are palpable, visible . . . perceived by all the senses."

From this prevailing optimism, however, it was often but a step to discontent, frustration, and anger. The doctrine of perfectability placed heavy strains on a society that exhibited many obvious imperfections. Americans might resent the facile strictures of some foreign visitors, but they could scarcely ignore the sharpening contrast between the ideals they professed and the realities with which they lived. Inveterate self-confidence therefore bred incessant self-criticism. Tocqueville arrived in the United States just a few months after William Lloyd Garrison published his first issue of *The Liberator*. A nation apparently preoccupied with material gain and the physical conquest of a continent was already entering its first great era of social reform.

The reform impulse was a natural corollary of the American democratic faith. It also absorbed strong influences from Europe, where the Enlightenment had partly secularized traditional religious imperatives. English utilitarianism exemplified the shift of philosophic attention from God to man, from salvation to human happiness, from sin to social injustice. A growing awareness of the connections between personal virtue and social environment compelled many Americans to reconsider some of their standard beliefs. For instance, they were awakening to the problem of poverty, a condition usually attributed either to the will of God or to lack of individual initiative. Misery was becoming more concentrated and visible in the crowded cities. Festering with disease and crime, slum districts like the notorious Five Points in New York provided convincing evidence that poverty, whatever its cause, could be a menace to the whole of society. In addition, the increasing amount of unemployment during periods of financial distress demonstrated that respectable men could be reduced to pauperism by forces beyond their control. Such were the paths to the discovery of social evil.

Exposure of serious defects in American society did not automatically win converts to reform, however. There remained the stout belief that a worthy man could overcome the handicaps of his environment and that the struggle would only strengthen his character. As the decades passed, this doctrine of individualism became identified more and more with conservative resistance to social action. On the other hand, certain groups chose to isolate themselves from the evils of the world and build their own better societies in miniature. Religious zeal was uppermost in many such communities, including those of the Shakers, the Rappites, the Perfectionists, and the Mormons. They bore a resemblance to the Puritans of early New England, who had hoped to erect a Zion in the wilderness. No less significant were the secular experiments in utopian socialism like the numerous Fourierist "phalanxes" and Robert Owen's community at New Harmony, Indiana. Most of these ventures quickly expired, but the enthusiasm that produced them was part of the general movement toward social reform.

There were two distinct kinds of reform impulse, although both frequently appeared in the same movement. One was the philanthropic and often self-righteous urge to remedy visible social ills, alleviate suffering, and discourage behavior that was considered immoral. The other was direct protest against alleged social injustice by people who regarded themselves as its victims. Philanthropic reform, originating primarily in the middle and upper classes, made somewhat better progress before the Civil War. Protest reform, springing from more populistic sources and slower to become articulate, did not reach its peak until late in the century. It was the humanitarian reformer, then, who emerged as a representative figure of the Jacksonian era.

Philanthropic reform characteristically gave its attention to the degraded elements of society whose conditions were a reproach to the nation—paupers, criminals, drunkards, insane and physically handicapped persons, orphans, slaves, Indians, and, in some respects, women. For example, the growing realization that jails and prisons served as schools in crime gradually produced revision of penal codes and improvement of penal institutions, with some enlightened emphasis upon reformation as well as punishment. Yet the slowness with which even the most successful movements made their progress is illustrated in the case of imprisonment for debt. This absurd legal custom began to encounter criticism shortly after the Revolution. Ameliorated in some states and first abolished by Kentucky in 1821, it did not disappear entirely until 1868.

Much of the resistance to reform was inertial and financial, but some movements provoked controversy of a more fundamental kind. Temperance crusaders, especially when they began to insist upon total abstinence and to supplement persuasion with demands for legal coercion, met strong opposition on the grounds that their proposals were sanctimonious, unrealistic, and inimical to personal liberty. Within the movement, there ensued a typical struggle between moderate and ultra factions, with the latter winning control. The crusade for temperance then became a crusade for prohibition. Maine enacted the first prohibitory statute in 1846. A dozen more states followed suit during the next decade, but two-thirds of these laws were soon repealed or declared unconstitutional.

Surpassing all other reform movements in its emotional force and disruptive effect was the crusade against slavery. Here, meliorative action would not satisfy humanitarian imperatives, since the institution in question was itself looked upon as inherently and utterly wrong. Whatever differences might arise over methods and timing, antislavery logic led to the ultimate objective of overthrowing a well-established social system. Philanthropic reform in this case became revolutionary.

The Missouri Compromise, by defining the limits of slavery expansion, had removed a dangerous issue from national politics, but meanwhile abolitionism was gaining support, and in the 1830s it emerged as an organized, aggressive movement. William Lloyd Garrison and other New Englanders joined with a New York group in 1833 to form the American Antislavery Society. Five years later, it claimed about 250,000 members in 1350 local units. There were close ties between abolitionism and Protestant evangelism, especially in Western states like Ohio, where Theodore Weld was the outstanding leader. Although they wasted much energy in quarrels among themselves, the abolitionists mounted a campaign of popular agitation that has seldom been equaled. From printing presses and platforms, in astonishing volume, poured their denunciation of slavery. Always a small minority, and widely detested even in the North, they had no visible effect upon the South except to harden its defenses. What they demanded was plainly impossible within the existing structure of the Republic, but that problem could wait; their immediate purpose was to awaken the conscience of America.

After 1836, when the gag rule and the Texas question renewed the slavery conflict in Congress, abolitionism moved toward political action. Despite vehement opposition from Garrison, who feared the corrupting environment of politics, the Liberty party was organized in 1839. It polled only 7000 votes in the presidential election of the following year. But then this was just the first antislavery political party, and there were others to come.

Many different kinds of people were drawn into the reform crusades of the era, and their motivation was often complex. It would be difficult to impugn the altruism of someone like Dorothea Dix, who devoted her whole life to humanitarian causes. Nevertheless, self-interest also played an important part, and some reformers obviously enjoyed such work because it satisfied their ambitions and absorbed their own feelings of frustration and aggression. But the reform movements were also an expression of national pride and aspiration—of the faith in America's special destiny. It was entirely appropriate that the wife of a leading reformer, herself the friend of many causes, should write "The Battle Hymn of the Republic."

EXPRESSION IN AMERICA

American reformers often drew strength from the knowledge that similar movements were in progress on the other side of the Atlantic. For example, British abolition of West Indian slavery in 1833 lent timely encouragement to American antislavery leaders. A half century after the Revolution, the United States remained a cultural dependency of Europe in many respects, notably in the realm of literary and artistic expression. This was by no means essentially unfortunate, since the raw young republic lacked the resources to build an indigenous civilization of decent quality. Inventive though Americans might be, they achieved their greatest triumphs by borrowing ideas and techniques from the old world and adapting them to the needs of the new. Yet tutelage, no matter how necessary, was a disagreeable condition, and the cry had long since been raised for the cultural independence that befitted a sovereign nation.

American art and literature in the nineteenth century followed the general European trend from neoclassicism to romanticism. These two styles are more easily labeled than identified and delimited. They overlapped in time, mixed with each other and with native elements, underwent local adaptation, and assumed different aspects in each medium of expression. The essence of classicism was rationality. It emphasized clarity and order, restraint and proportion, felicity and elegance. Romanticism, in contrast, had an eruptive quality. It elevated intuition above reason and sacrified regularity of form for intensity of feeling. Its mood was exuberantly rebellious, and it drew inspiration from nature, from faraway places, and from the medieval tradition. Classicism could shrivel into sterile formalism, while romanticism at its worst became grotesque and maudlin. The two styles were antipathetical, and yet not entirely so, for both sprang from the same desire to ennoble man by leading him toward beauty and truth.

Classical influences were perhaps most conspicuous in American architecture of the early nineteenth century. The dominant "Federal style"— represented in the national Capitol, the White House, and Jefferson's Monticello—imitated or adapted Roman forms and Renaissance translations thereof. It seemed appropriate for the United States to model its buildings after those of the great ancient republic, and Jefferson in particular hoped to develop an architecture that would symbolize the ideals and aspirations of the new nation. While embodying the classical virtues of symmetry and restraint, the Federal style, with its domes, colonnaded porticoes, and balustrades, was an expression of urbane taste and sometimes achieved a "decorative splendor." By 1820, however, the classic revival was passing from its Roman to its Greek phase. Here, a simpler and more severe concept of beauty prevailed. Gracious curves were replaced by straight lines, and all embellishment was concentrated in the huge prostyle, with heavy columns and crowning pediment, which extended across the entire front of a building. Every edifice from privy to statehouse, said one sarcastic observer, had to be a replica of a Greek temple.

By about 1840, the Greek style was losing favor except in the South, where it continued to symbolize the patrician values of the plantation aristocracy. Medieval Gothic had already emerged as an expression of the romantic spirit. Classical symmetry gave way to picturesque irregularity of form with soaring vertical lines that radically changed the urban skyline. The spires, turrets, and battlements of the Gothic style could be arranged with infinite variety, and they summoned up sentimental remembrance of the age of faith and chivalry. Yet classicism did not disappear from American architecture. Its influence remained especially strong in the designing of public buildings, as any tour of capital cities will reveal. In Washington today, the medieval red towers of the Smithsonian Institution (actually more Romanesque than Gothic) stand out in sharp contrast to the overwhelmingly predominant classical style.

Dependence on Europe was manifest, though far from uniform, in all of the fine arts. Americans of the nineteenth century made scarcely any significant contributions to serious music, except as patrons. No native composer achieved distinction, and the leading performers came from abroad on provincial tour. For sculpture too, in Jefferson's time, Europeans were preferred as a matter of course and received the important commissions. The first group of truly professional American sculptors—including Horatio Greenough, Hiram Powers, and Thomas Crawford—appeared during the

Trinity Church, New York City, a fine example of the Gothic Revival.

One of the most famous American landscape paintings, Thomas Cole's "The Oxbow" (Connecticut River near Northampton), 1846.

1830s, but they studied and did most of their work in Italy. Their statuary, as a consequence, helped perpetuate the classical style in the United States. Greenough, the most original artist in the group, was better appreciated by later generations than by his own, whereas Powers won excessive but impermanent acclaim for his vapid nude, "The Greek Slave."

American painting was much further advanced. The Revolutionary generation had produced a group of professional artists who spent extensive periods in England and settled there permanently in some cases. Younger men like Washington Allston and Samuel Morse also went abroad for training, but were less inclined to become expatriates. Portraiture remained popular, being the best way to earn a living, and so did historical themes, but the romantic influence is evident in a growing preference for nature as a subject. Allston's landscapes, together with those of Thomas Cole and the "Hudson River school," captured the mood of romanticism not only in their themes but in their emotional content. Even portrait painting, within the limits imposed by the necessity of producing an accurate likeness, began to communicate the humane sentiment and inner passion of the romantic movement.

Artistic expression in America was most derivative at the higher levels of culture, where only Europe could provide adequate technical training.

But the artistic impulse did not confine itself to the ranks of professionals. A folk culture embracing music, sculpture, painting, and fine handicrafts dated far back into the colonial period and was more deeply rooted in native soil. Vernacular art, such as textile designs and the carved figureheads on sailing vessels, often merged decorative with utilitarian purposes and made

"Baltimore Orioles," one of the plates in John James Audubon's *The Birds of America.*

its own way, refreshingly heedless of the canons of cultivated taste. Further-more, the challenge of technology absorbed much creative energy in America. Machines, tools, and buildings reflected an emphasis on lightness and economy, on flexibility and efficiency. The durability demanded by Europeans received less consideration, with the fortunate result that obsolescence was minimized in American technology. Some achievements, like the "balloon-frame" house (about 1833) which substituted two-by-four studs for much heavier timbers, were utterly utilitarian and aesthetically deplorable. Yet one also finds science and art triumphantly fused in the graceful clipper ships and in John James Audubon's *The Birds of America*.

It was literature, above all, that Americans had in mind when they called for cultural independence, but the achievements of the post-Revolutionary generation fell far short of expectations. The young nation did not yet have sufficient intellectual and institutional foundations on which to build a separate literary tradition, and the ties of a common language bound it closely to English modes. Even when they adopted native themes, American writers tended to imitate Pope or Swift or Addison. They also suffered financially from the competition of British works, pirated by American publishers for a reading public that still looked to Europe as the only source of serious literature. As a consequence, promising young men like the novelist Charles Brockden Brown and the lyric poet Philip Freneau turned to commerce and journalism in order to make a living.

The hopes of early literary nationalists could not be realized until the instruments of culture were sufficient to produce trained writers, sensitive critics, and receptive readers. More time was needed for the growth of schools and colleges, libraries and theaters, newspapers, magazines, and publishing houses. It was not just accident that six of the greatest figures in American literature were born within sixteen years of each other during the first two decades of the nineteenth century.* They reached maturity at a propitious time. In 1837, when Ralph Waldo Emerson stirred his Phi Beta Kappa audience with the words, "Let the passion for America cast out the passion for Europe," he was renewing an old plea that had ceased to be premature.

As the turning point, one might well designate the years 1819 to 1821,

---

* Ralph Waldo Emerson (1803), Nathaniel Hawthorne (1804), Edgar Allan Poe (1809), Henry David Thoreau (1817), Herman Melville (1819), Walt Whitman (1819). The list could be lengthened with names like William Gilmore Simms (1806), Henry Wadsworth Longfellow (1807), John Greenleaf Whittier (1807), Oliver Wendell Holmes (1809), and James Russell Lowell (1819).

when Washington Irving published his *Sketchbook* of essays and stories, when William Cullen Bryant's first collection of poems appeared, and when James Fenimore Cooper, after one false start, won acclaim for *The Spy,* a novel set in the Revolutionary period. Irving, the first American man of letters to earn an international reputation, combined the urbane charm and wit of the neoclassic manner with the sentiment and misty nostalgia of an emerging romanticism. Bryant, too, in his intensely personal poetry of nature, was a gentle herald of the romantic movement. Cooper, fusing romanticism with the frontier in his Leatherstocking series, created the first great fictional hero in American literature and, in doing so, made a significant contribution to national myth.

The romantic impulse, being of European origin, tended in some respects to prolong the period of American literary tutelage, but by nature it was essentially a liberating influence. Blending well with the spirit of nationalism and democracy, romanticism placed too much stress upon individual feeling and imagination to be anything but subversive of prescribed patterns, even its own. There was, to be sure, much imitative homage to Wordsworth, Scott, and Byron, but the great men of the era were bold and free spirits who assimilated the romantic temper to their own artistic needs.

None was bolder or freer than Emerson—essayist, poet, and teacher who summoned men to cast off the bonds of tradition and embrace the universe directly through the power of intuitive insight. Emerson was more than a leader of the New England transcendentalists, that diverse and yet congenial group of intellectuals who translated the romantic movement into peculiarly American terms. He served as the chief prophet of an age that sensed the opportunity for renaissance, for new beginnings in a new land. This was the poetic version of manifest destiny.

In Walt Whitman, Emerson immediately recognized a kindred spirit, despite their many differences. Whitman's poetry, richly sensuous and exuberantly freed of all formal literary restraints, was the ultimate celebration of individualism and democracy in the American setting. *Leaves of Grass,* first published in 1855 but revised many times thereafter, became the fountainhead of American poetry for the next several generations.

There were also writers of tragic vision who explored the darker side of man's experience, confronted the problem of evil, and cried out against fate. But it was only the twentieth-century American who could truly appreciate Melville's genius or fully understand Hawthorne's. The prevailing optimism of the younger Republic was in tune with the affirmations, demanding rather than complacent, of Emerson and Whitman.

Chapter VII

The Transcontinental Republic

DEMOCRACY AND DESTINY

For a generation after the acquisition of Florida, the boundaries of the United States remained unchanged. In the 1820s, some men grumbled about the "surrender" of claims to Texas, but it was now unquestionably a part of Mexico. The arrangement with England for joint occupation of Oregon continued in force, but that far country was controlled by the Hudson's Bay Company, and few Americans took much interest in it. Occupation of the Mississippi Valley was absorbing the pioneering energies of the nation. Beyond its fertile lands stretched the treeless Great Plains, misnamed the "Great American Desert" and soon to be designated permanent Indian Country. Beyond that lay the forbidding ranges of the Rocky Mountains, which many Americans were willing to accept as the ultimate limits of the Republic.

Nevertheless, a few vanguards of the frontier were already penetrating the Far West during the 1820s, while American settlers had begun to cross the international boundary into Texas. Meanwhile, the public domain of the United States, although still vast, was shrinking noticeably every year, and the procession of new states into the Union confirmed the impression that the country was filling up with astonishing speed. The aggressive spirit of national expansionism, never entirely dormant, grew stronger in the 1830s and burst forth to dominate the history of the 1840s. By that time, the American people had evolved a set of ideas to explain and justify the mood of expansion. One of the phrases that eventually appeared in their turgid rhetoric was "manifest destiny," which has since become a convenient label for the whole complex of attitudes, concepts, and actions that swept American dominion to the shores of the Pacific Ocean.

There is no clear line between the actual reasons and the rationalizations for expansion in the 1840s. Any list of fundamental causes and motives should probably include the land hunger of American pioneers and their habitual readiness to migrate, the desire for commercial bases on the Pacific like San Francisco Bay, a soaring national pride that could easily be translated into belligerence, and a determination to prevent new European encroachments on the North American continent. But to justify expansion, the editors, politicians, and other spokesmen turned also to political and pseudoscientific theory. They adopted the biological analogy that a nation must grow like an organism. They embraced geographical determinism in arguing that the "natural" western boundary of the United States was obviously the Pacific Ocean. They claimed a natural right to land for those people who made "superior use" of the soil. At the heart of manifest destiny, however, was an exuberant faith in the democratic creed. Americans, said the prophets of westward expansion, were virtually a chosen race, and their appointed mission was to extend the "area of freedom."

THE EARLY FAR WEST

The first Americans to visit the Far West did so from the sea. Sailing vessels, engaged in the China trade and in the hunting of otters and seals, were making calls at various places on the Pacific coast by the 1790s. A New England captain, Robert Gray, explored and named the Columbia River in 1792. John Jacob Astor established a fur-trading post at the mouth of that stream in 1811, but the onset of war with Great Britain forced him to withdraw the following year. During the 1820s, a thriving trade in cattle hides and tallow sprang up between California and New England ports. Some agents of American mercantile houses took up permanent residence in the drowsy Mexican province, and soon they were dominating its commercial life.

Overland exploration of the Far West began with the famous journey of Meriwether Lewis and William Clark in 1804–1806. Leading a party of about fifty men, they followed the Missouri River to its headwaters, then found their way through mountain passes to the lower Columbia and continued down that stream to the Pacific coast. They returned by approximately the same route, but separated for a time so that Clark could explore the length of the Yellowstone River. The Lewis and Clark adventure was the first of several Western expeditions sent out by the federal government to map the country, gather scientific data, and impress the Indians. For the most part, however, these official explorers, like Zebulon Pike and Stephen H. Long, failed to penetrate the Rocky Mountain barrier. Not until the efforts of John C. Frémont in the 1840s did government exploration again approach the scale of the Lewis and Clark achievement.

The Western trapper, idealized by the American painter, Charles Deas, in the Yale University Art Gallery.

The major work of exploration was performed by the fur trappers, who began to move far up the Missouri as early as 1807 and, by the 1820s, were roaming over large parts of the Far West in search of beaver. These adventurous and often half-savage "mountain men" spied out the passes, valleys, and streams, established the first crude trails, and carried word of their discoveries back to the frontier settlements. Some of them, like the intrepid Jedediah Strong Smith, who led the first overland expedition of Americans into California, met death from hostile Indians and other hazards of the wilderness. Others, like Kit Carson and Jim Bridger, survived to act as army scouts and wagon-train guides in a later day. Excessive trapping soon made the beaver scarce and ended the brief era of the mountain men, but not before they had opened the Far West in spectacular fashion.

A different kind of enterprise, begun in the 1820s, linked the American frontier with the old Spanish borderlands of the Southwest. This was the trade between Missouri and Santa Fe, carried on by wagon trains that plodded westward to exchange a variety of goods for New Mexican silver, furs, and mules. By the early 1840s, annual shipments were worth nearly a half million dollars, and the wagons had marked out the important Santa Fe Trail, soon to become a highway of American conquest.

Also in the vanguard of American movement toward the Pacific were the missionaries who entered Oregon country during the 1830s. A Methodist, Jason Lee, was the first to arrive. Welcomed by John McLoughlin, chief factor of the Hudson's Bay Company, he established himself in the Willamette Valley, and his mission became the nucleus of a small American settlement. A little later, Marcus Whitman and a few associates built a mission farther inland near the bend of the Columbia. Supported by the Presbyterian and Congregational churches, this venture was beset with troubles, and it ended tragically in 1847 when the Cayuse Indians slaughtered Whitman, his wife, and a dozen other residents. Meanwhile, before 1840, the Americans in Oregon had begun asking the United States to take formal possession of the region. Their petitions received little attention in Congress, but the "Oregon question" had made its entry into national politics.

THE TEXAS REPUBLIC

There was also a "Texas question" confronting political leaders by the 1840s. It had begun to take shape in 1821, when a Missourian named Moses Austin received a grant from Spanish authorities in Mexico permitting him to colonize 300 families on Texas land. Before the year ended, however, Mexican independence had been won and Austin was dead. His son Stephen organized the actual settlement, persuading the Mexican government to confirm the grant and subsequently enlarge it. Soon the Austin colony, centered on the Brazos River, numbered several thousand American pioneers, most of them Southerners and all attracted by the opportunity to obtain virtually free land in the amount of one square league per family. Pleased with the results, Mexico authorized grants to other *"empresarios."* New settlers continued to arrive at such a rate that the immigrant population of Texas probably exceeded 25,000 in 1825.

Austin sincerely intended to be a loyal Mexican citizen, and he demonstrated his allegiance in 1826 by opposing the abortive "Fredonian Revolt" of Haden Edwards. Yet the Americans entering Texas obviously constituted an alien element within the Republic of Mexico. They were predominantly non-Catholic, spoke a different language, demanded a large measure of local autonomy, and ignored or circumvented the Mexican law forbidding slavery. Many of them were habitually unruly and openly contemptuous of Spanish institutions. As Mexico's uneasiness about Texas increased, so did her suspicion that the United States had designs upon the province. Efforts to tighten control and terminate immigration only made the Texans more restless. A radical minority began to advocate independence, and its hand was strengthened by the menacing attitude of Antonio Lopez de Santa Anna, the new Mexican dictator. In 1835, he dispatched troops to certain points in Texas and issued a decree abolishing the federal system. With clashes occurring between Texans and Mexican soldiers, the situation now bore some resemblance to that of the American colonies in 1775.

Early in 1836, Santa Anna led a large army into Texas, determined to crush the incipient rebellion. He wiped out the little garrison at the Alamo in San Antonio and slaughtered more than 300 Americans who surrendered at Goliad. Meanwhile, a convention of Texans had issued a declaration of independence on March 1. The provisional government appointed Samuel Houston, friend of Andrew Jackson and onetime governor of Tennessee, to command the revolutionary army. Houston first retreated before the advancing Mexican force, then turned and smashed it in the decisive battle of San Jacinto on April 21. Santa Anna was taken prisoner and signed a treaty—later repudiated—pledging recognition of Texan independence. In October 1836, Houston became the first president of the new republic.

Realizing the hazards of independence in the face of continued Mexican hostility, the Texans promptly requested annexation to the United States. But President Jackson suppressed his personal feelings and assumed a very cautious attitude, even delaying formal recognition of Texas until March 1837. Hasty annexation would belie the American government's pose of neutrality in the Texas Revolution and probably bring on a war with Mexico. Furthermore, there was strong opposition in the Northeast to the acquisition of Texas, largely on antislavery grounds. The issue, if pressed in Congress, would surely precipitate a bitter sectional controversy. It might even disrupt the Democratic party. And so the Van Buren administration, like its predecessor, waited and watched while Texas fretfully withdrew the request for annexation and charted an independent course in international affairs.

NEW FRONTIERS OF THE 1840s

In 1840, there was still a frontier at the northern end of the Mississippi Valley. Most of Iowa and Wisconsin were still unsettled, and only a few people had advanced into Minnesota. The occupation of this attractive region absorbed the energies of many pioneers during the decade of manifest destiny. Farther south, however, the westward movement had reached the edge of the "permanent" Indian country. Rather than press forward into an area that was physically uninviting and legally closed to settlement, restless farmers turned their eyes toward faraway Oregon and California.

A wagon train at South Pass in Wyoming, sketched by William Henry Jackson.

The overland migrations to the Pacific Coast had begun by 1841, when 69 men, women, and children set out from Independence, Missouri, along the Oregon Trail. They followed the Platte River to South Pass in what is now western Wyoming, crossed the Green River, and headed for the valley of the Snake. Just before reaching that stream, however, the party divided. About half of the emigrants continued on the difficult but more or less familiar route to Oregon; the others turned southwest into the Humboldt Desert and struggled across the towering Sierra Nevada to the San Joaquin Valley of California. In succeeding years, the volume of migration increased to more than a thousand persons annually. Some of them preferred California, but a majority followed the Snake and Columbia rivers to the Willamette Valley, which seemed the more likely to become a part of the United States.

The steady procession of covered wagons into Oregon obviously strengthened American claims to that remote region, which for a generation had been dominated by the Hudson's Bay Company. This meant that the joint-occupation agreement was now working in favor of the United States, and that it would be advantageous to postpone the day of final settlement with

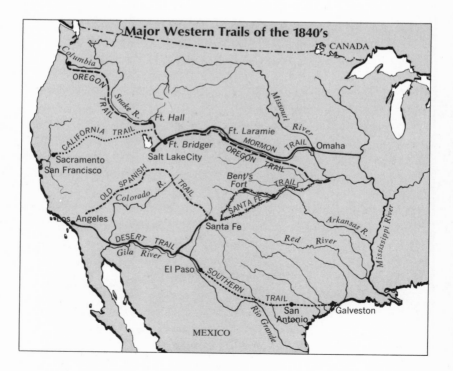

Major Western Trails of the 1840's

Great Britain. The Oregon pioneers, however, wanted the protection of American sovereignty, especially in order to secure clear land titles. When Congress failed to act, they organized their own provisional government in 1843, but continued to clamor for annexation.

Meanwhile, the overland pioneers in California were making their presence felt. Numbering about 300 by 1845, these people contrasted sharply with earlier American arrivals. Agriculture, not commerce, was their primary interest; they came from the Mississippi Valley instead of the Atlantic seaboard; they were less cosmopolitan and therefore less tolerant of Spanish culture; and they settled in the unpopulated interior valleys rather than on the coast. Mexican authorities, remembering the lesson of Texas, watched them with growing suspicion, and the immigrants in turn became increasingly apprehensive about their status in the province. From this mutual mistrust, it was only a short step to open conflict.

To pioneers bound for Oregon and California, the arid intermontane region beyond the Rockies seemed grimly unsuitable for habitation. Yet its very desolateness served to attract a unique group of settlers in the 1840s. Joseph Smith and his Latter-Day Saints, driven out of Missouri, had established themselves in 1839 at Nauvoo, Illinois, on the banks of the Mississippi. There, within a few years, these remarkable people built a flourishing community, but they also aroused the animosity of non-Mormons in the vicinity. Violence erupted in 1844, and Smith was murdered by a mob. To his successor, Brigham Young, it soon became painfully clear that the Saints must once again abandon their homes and seek a new refuge from persecution. The exodus began in February, 1846, when advance parties crossed the frozen Mississippi. By the end of that year, about 12,000 Mormons had made the journey through Iowa to winter quarters built on the west side of the Missouri River. Then, in the spring of 1847, Young led a "pioneer band" westward along the Oregon Trail. They did not know their destination until they saw it—the valley of Great Salt Lake, a desert that could be made to bloom by irrigation. Promising security because of its isolation, this new Zion was outside the boundaries of the United States, but not for long.

THE POLITICS OF EXPANSION

It was during the administration of John Tyler, the first accidental president, that territorial expansion came to the fore as an issue in American politics. Virtually expelled from the Whig party as a result of his quarrel with

Clay, Tyler had little opportunity for effective leadership except in the conduct of foreign policy. And there, as it turned out, he was setting the stage for more spectacular achievements by his successor.

The Webster-Ashburton Treaty of 1842, for example, disposed of several troublesome issues with England, especially the quarrel over the boundary between Maine and New Brunswick. Although the agreement did not cover the Oregon question, it helped clear the air for a peaceful settlement of that controversy. Webster, who clung for a time to his post as Secretary of State after other Whig leaders had resigned from the Tyler cabinet, also worked out a plan for the acquisition of California, but his efforts came to nothing. In any case, Tyler's principal ambition was to secure the annexation of Texas. Americans were now showing more concern about the Texas Republic because of indications that it might be drawn into close association with Great Britain. Tyler scented in this rising interest an opportunity to win popular support for himself and perhaps even reelection.

At the same time, Texas leaders were ready to renew their request for annexation. A heavy debt burdened the young republic; Mexico still refused to recognize its independence; and an effort in 1841 to seize control of the Santa Fe region had ended disastrously. The Tyler administration therefore negotiated a treaty of annexation without much difficulty and submitted it to the Senate in the spring of 1844. However, the treaty was partly the work of Calhoun, who had just become the new Secretary of State, and this lent strength to antislavery attacks upon it. Furthermore, with the presidential campaign getting under way, Texas was now a partisan issue. Whig senators stood almost unanimously against annexation, and they were joined by some Democrats of the Van Buren wing. The treaty, as a consequence, met overwhelming defeat. Texas once again found itself rejected.

At the beginning of 1844, it was generally expected that Clay and Van Buren would be the presidential nominees of their respective parties. Both men were cool toward expansionism, and late in April, probably by prior agreement, they issued statements more or less opposing the annexation of Texas. The Whig convention did nominate Clay, but the Democrats surprised everyone, including themselves. Van Buren's pronouncement had alienated many Southerners and Westerners. The ex-President led on the first ballot but failed to get the two-thirds majority required by convention rules. After that, he lost ground, and the contest became a deadlock that was finally broken by the nomination of James K. Polk, a late entry in the contest. This party stalwart, formerly Speaker of the House of Representatives and Governor of

Tennessee, had the blessing of Andrew Jackson. He was also an ardent expansionist, completely in sympathy with a platform that called for "the reoccupation of Oregon and the reannexation of Texas."

Clay, although far better known than his opponent, had been outmaneuvered on the Texas question, and no amount of subsequent hedging could convince expansionists that he was in step with them. In addition, Tyler gave up plans to run as an independent and joined forces with Polk, while the candidacy of James G. Birney, nominated by the abolitionist Liberty party, promised to draw off more Whigs than Democrats. Yet the election proved to be one of the closest in American history. Clay lost New York, and with it the presidency, by a mere 5000 votes. The abolitionists of that state, in casting almost 16,000 ballots for Birney, had nudged Polk into the White House.

Accepting the results of the election as a personal vindication, Tyler was determined to end his administration on a note of triumph by bringing Texas into the Union. He proposed to do so by securing passage of a joint resolution in both houses of Congress. This expedient would circumvent the requirement of a two-thirds vote in the Senate for ratification of a treaty. Despite doubts about its constitutionality, the desired resolution was passed, and Tyler, just before leaving office, formally invited Texas to become a state. After the necessary arrangements were made by the Polk administration, Texas finally entered the Union on December 29, 1845.

COMPROMISE AND CONFLICT

Not only younger but more obscure than any previous winner of a presidential election, James K. Polk was nevertheless a man of clear purpose and strong will. Few political leaders have attained their stated objectives so completely or with such speed. In his domestic policies, Polk proved to be a strict constructionist and an unyielding opponent of Clay's American system. By securing reestablishment of the Independent Treasury, which the Whigs had abolished in 1841, he dealt another blow to forlorn advocates of a national bank. At the same time, protectionists were discomfited. The Walker tariff of 1846 lowered duties substantially and resumed the trend toward free trade that had been interrupted by a Whig tariff in 1842. The principal opposition to these two measures came from the Northeast, but when Polk also stubbornly vetoed river-and-harbor legislation, he antagonized

Whigs and Democrats alike in the Northwest. These actions increased the strain upon Democratic unity and made the President increasingly vulnerable to the charge that he was a willing tool of the slave power.

Polk entered the White House publicly committed on the Oregon and Texas issues, as well as privately determined to acquire California. During previous administrations, the Oregon dispute had been narrowed, with Great Britain offering to surrender the region south of the Columbia River, while the United States proposed a division at the 49th parallel. In the campaign of 1844, however, the Democratic platform had asserted American title to the "whole" of Oregon—that is, all the way up to the southern boundary of Russian Alaska at 54°40'. Polk's obligation, as a consequence, was not entirely clear. He began by making another offer to compromise on the 49th parallel. When that met rejection, he shifted to a more belligerent attitude and announced that the United States would now defend its claim to the whole territory. With the cry "54°40' or fight" echoing across the country, Congress in April 1846 passed a resolution authorizing termination of the agreement for joint occupation. The Oregon controversy had reached the stage of crisis.

Yet the two nations were by now accustomed to settling their disputes peacefully, and neither really wanted to force a military showdown over Oregon. At this very time, the proposed Walker tariff and the impending repeal of English corn laws promised to strengthen their commercial ties. In addition, American aggressiveness was tempered by the imminence of war with Mexico. The British government made the principal concession by offering, for the first time, to accept the 49th parallel as the line of division. Polk took the unusual precaution of obtaining the Senate's prior sanction before signing the treaty and presenting it formally to that body. Despite the bitter opposition of 54°40' irreconcilables from the Old Northwest, the treaty was approved on June 18, 1846, by a vote of 41 to 14. Called a compromise, it was in truth a negotiated victory for the United States.

The Texas problem, in one sense, had already been solved when Polk entered the White House. He needed only to carry forward the program initiated by Tyler. The Mexican government, however, insisted that annexation was an act of war and broke off diplomatic relations with the United States. This issue alone might have been settled peacefully, but there were additional reasons for the crisis that ensued.

Most important, Polk endorsed the extravagant claim of Texas to all territory north and east of the Rio Grande, although its southern boundary

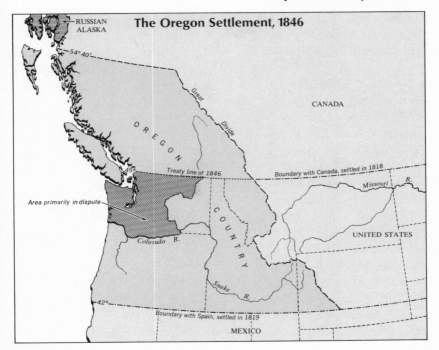

The Oregon Settlement, 1846

RUSSIAN ALASKA

54° 40'

Great Divide

CANADA

OREGON

49°

Treaty line of 1846

Boundary with Canada, settled in 1818

Missouri R.

Area primarily in dispute

COUNTRY

Colorado R.

UNITED STATES

Snake R.

42°

Boundary with Spain, settled in 1819

MEXICO

as a Mexican state had been the Nueces River. Thus, while the whole of Texas remained in dispute between the United States and Mexico, the region south of the Nueces became the focus of conflict. Early in 1846, Polk ordered troops under General Zachary Taylor to advance and take a position along the Rio Grande. If one considers the state of tension and the weakness of the American case, it is difficult not to conclude that this was the deliberately provocative act of a man who saw opportunity rather than danger in the mounting crisis.

Meanwhile, the President also had his eye on California. That province, remote and loosely controlled from Mexico City, seemed increasingly available for the taking, and Polk's course of action was influenced by the fear that it might fall into British hands. American efforts to buy at least part of California, including the magnificent harbor of San Francisco, dated from Jackson's second administration. Polk likewise offered to purchase the province, but Mexican officials, already convinced that they were being robbed of Texas, had no intention of yielding more territory to the hated Yankee.

The President, in any case, was promoting acquisition by another method. Some of the leading Spanish Californians tended to favor American annexation, and with their help a peaceful transfer might be arranged. Polk detailed Thomas O. Larkin, the United States consul at Monterey, as his secret agent in the delicate negotiations. Larkin was proceeding with considerable success when an unexpected incident changed the whole situation. The restless pioneers in the Sacramento Valley, encouraged by the presence of John C. Frémont with a sizable exploring party, decided to seize the initiative. Capturing the little pueblo of Sonoma on June 14, 1846, they proclaimed the Bear Flag Republic. Thus armed revolt superseded the plans for peaceful transfer, but soon the revolutionary movement was itself absorbed by American military conquest.

In Mexico, amid continuing political disorder, there was growing sentiment for war with the United States. Government officials had refused to receive an American envoy in December 1845, and they proclaimed their intention to defend every inch of Mexican territory. Late in April 1846, Mexican troops crossed the Rio Grande and attacked Taylor's forces, only to be thrown back after two weeks of hard fighting. Polk, upon receiving word of these hostilities, drew up a war message in which he asserted that Mexico had "shed American blood upon the American soil." His case was dubious at best, but Congress responded on May 11–12 with a declaration of war.

THE WAR WITH MEXICO

The conflict that ensued became a major turning point in American history. It was the nation's first foreign war, and the decisive campaign involved the military forces in their first large-scale amphibious operation. Clearly a war of conquest, despite excuses to the contrary, it marked the culmination of aggressive expansionism. Yet the triumph over Mexico raised issues that put an end to national expansion and introduced a new era of ominous sectional strife. In addition, the remoteness of battle and the apparent easiness of victory may have led the American people to regard war itself too lightly.

Neither nation was adequately prepared for the military action that its belligerent policies required. Mexico had the larger number of men under arms and would be fighting on the defensive, but these advantages were canceled by the low quality of leadership, morale, and equipment, as well as the vulnerability of her thinly-populated northern provinces. The regular army of the United States, although well officered, amounted to a skeleton force of less than 8000 men. Its size increased substantially as the war progressed, but the government depended primarily upon short-term volunteers. These were often unreliable, and their early enthusiasm tended to wane. The superiority of American field artillery weighed heavily in battle. Primitive sanitary conditions, slow communications, and the long supply lines constituted the most serious handicaps. For every American soldier killed in action, six died of disease.

Polk's aggressive expansionism manifested itself as soon as the war began. He ordered Colonel Stephen W. Kearny to lead an "Army of the West" into New Mexico and then on to California. In July 1846, while Kearny's troops were marching westward along the Santa Fe Trail, United States naval forces in the Pacific seized Monterey and San Francisco. Commodore Robert F. Stockton, enlisting the services of Frémont and the Bear Flaggers, met little resistance as he swiftly completed the occupation of California. The real fighting began late in September, when the populace of Los Angeles staged a successful revolt against the inadequate American garrison. For several months, the rebels gave a good account of themselves, and much of southern California returned to Mexican control. Kearny, having taken Santa Fe, arrived on the scene in December with a token force of 100 men. He and Stockton soon recaptured Los Angeles, and by the middle of January, California was peaceful again.

Meanwhile, Taylor had begun the invasion of northern Mexico, taking Monterey in September 1846. There, to Polk's displeasure, he negotiated an eight-week armistice. Democratic leaders were, in any case, becoming worried about Taylor's popularity at home and the talk among Whigs of making him their next presidential candidate. Thus a combination of military and political considerations prompted Polk to accept the plan of General Winfield Scott for a landing in force on the Gulf coast of Mexico. Two-thirds of Taylor's troops were transferred to the expedition, just as he faced a strong counterattack. The irrepressible Santa Anna, about to become the Mexican president again, was marching northward with an army of 15,000 men. At the hard-fought battle of Buena Vista in February 1847, the outnumbered Americans won a decisive victory. That ended the serious fighting in northern Mexico.

In March 1847, Scott landed his invasion army of about 10,000 men

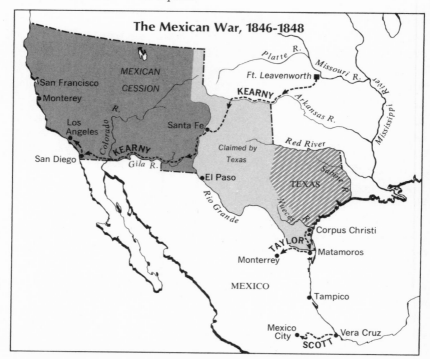

The Mexican War, 1846-1848

on the beaches south of Vera Cruz. He captured that city after a brief siege and then began his march westward toward the capital. After leaving the coastal plain, the route became difficult, winding steeply upward to a high plateau. At the first mountain pass, the Cerro Gordo, hard fighting and an enveloping operation overcame Mexican opposition. The advance paused from August 27 to September 7 while peace terms were discussed and rejected. Then Scott's army moved forward again. On September 14, following several more engagements, the American flag was raised in Mexico City.

The war was now virtually won, but bringing it to a formal close did not prove easy. Santa Anna, after a vain attempt to organize further resistance, fled the country, and peace negotiations waited until a new government was formed. Ever since May, Nicholas P. Trist had been on hand as Polk's special diplomatic representative, authorized to conclude a peace treaty. In November, however, Trist received notice of his recall. More time elapsed before he boldly decided to proceed with negotiations in defiance of his orders. Finally, in the Treaty of Guadalupe Hidalgo signed on February 2,

1848, Mexico not only surrendered Texas but ceded California and New Mexico to the United States. The United States, in turn, agreed to pay $15 million and assume claims of its citizens against the Mexican government. Despite its dubious origins and the opposition of a vocal minority that wanted to annex all of Mexico, the treaty was accepted by Polk and won approval in the Senate. Including Texas, about 1.2 million square miles had been added to the national domain.

1848 AND AFTER

The Mexican War had scarcely begun before its implications began to shift the course of American history. In August 1846, Polk requested $2 million for use in peace negotiations. To the appropriation bill, Congressman David Wilmot of Pennsylvania attached an amendment providing that there should be no slavery in any territory obtained from Mexico. Clearly, the strong support given the Wilmot Proviso amounted to much more than an antislavery maneuver. It was in part an effort by Whigs and embittered Van Buren Democrats to embarrass the Polk administration. It also reflected dissatisfaction in the Northeast with the Walker tariff, and in the Northwest with the Oregon compromise and Polk's stubborn opposition to internal improvements legislation. The Proviso movement, in short, was an attack not merely upon the institution of slavery, but upon the political power of the slavery interest, and as such, it constituted a declaration of political war.

John C. Calhoun responded for the South early in 1847 with a series of resolutions declaring that Congress, as the mere agent of the states, had no power to prohibit slavery in the federal territories. Thus positions taken during the Mexican War foreshadowed the confrontation between the Republican party and the slaveholding South in 1860 and 1861. The Wilmot Proviso and Calhoun's counterattack both repudiated the traditional method of adjusting the slavery issue to westward expansion, and it became increasingly apparent that the controversy could not be settled by extending the Missouri-Compromise line to the Pacific. Instead, a new formula for sectional conciliation was needed, and two were put forward. One, the principle of "popular sovereignty," would permit the residents of a territory to make their own choice between legalizing and prohibiting slavery. On the other hand, if the whole matter were treated as a strictly constitutional question, it could be left to the ultimate disposition of the Supreme Court. Neither of these solutions, one excessively democratic and the other a circumvention of the democratic process, actually incorporated a settlement of the substantive issue. Both were essentially evasions rather than compromises, shifting the responsibility from Congress to another authority. Each served only to postpone the day of decision, and the last futile effort at compromise in 1860 was a return to the old, discredited formula of drawing a line between slavery and freedom.

The House of Representatives, with a decided Northern majority, approved the Wilmot Proviso in 1846, but the Senate failed to take any action on it before adjournment of the session. Again in 1847, the House attached the Proviso to an appropriation bill, and this time the Senate formally rejected it. The stalemate in Congress continued and became more critical when the war ended and the need arose for civil government in the territory acquired from Mexico. California was an especially urgent case.

Californians were already growing restless under military rule when a dramatic event transformed their circumstances and intensified the sectional controversy. In January 1848, just a few days before Nicholas Trist signed the Treaty of Guadalupe Hidalgo, gold was discovered on the American River near Sacramento. The rush that followed did not reach its peak until the following year, when nearly 100,000 treasure seekers poured into the province from many parts of the world. The size and character of this new population made stable government imperative and greatly increased the pressure upon Congress. California must soon be organized as a territory or admitted as a state.

Meanwhile, the problem of slavery in the territories had become the dominant issue in the political campaign of 1848. Both major parties more or less evaded the dangerous question not only in their official platforms but in choosing their presidential candidates. The Democrats nominated Lewis Cass of Michigan, who had personally endorsed the principle of popular sovereignty. The Whigs, turning again to a war hero, selected Zachary Taylor, a Southerner without political experience, who took no stand on the slavery issue. These nominations were unacceptable to many antislavery Democrats and Whigs. Joining forces with members of the Liberty party, the rebellious elements organized the Free Soil party. Their platform, which supported free homesteads and internal improvements as well as the Wilmot Proviso, was remarkably similar to the one that the Republicans would write in 1860. The idealism of the Free Soil movement lost some of its luster, however, when that timeworn political veteran, Martin Van Buren, received the party's nomination for the presidency.

The presidential election of 1848 was another exceedingly close contest. Cass carried eight free and seven slave states with 127 electoral votes. Taylor carried seven free and eight slave states with 163 electoral votes. Van Buren, while getting about 10 percent of the popular vote, failed to win a single state. Nevertheless, his candidacy drew off enough Democrats in New York to give Taylor his victory.

On the surface, it appeared that the slavery problem had not seriously disturbed the equilibrium of parties and sections in American politics. For the third time in a row, the opposition had captured the presidency. Whig and Democratic strength was relatively equal not only in the nation as a whole but in both the North and the South. The political sectionalism of the Free Soilers seemed to be a failure. Yet the persistence of the territorial controversy in Congress soon demonstrated that Proviso sentiment had not diminished and that the election had settled nothing.

The expected closeness of the election in 1848 deterred many free soil sympathizers from wasting their votes on Van Buren. After their devastating defeat four years later, discouraged Northern Whigs would be more susceptible to the appeal of a sectional party. Furthermore, the antislavery forces in 1846 to 1848 were pressing the attack upon the South, and this

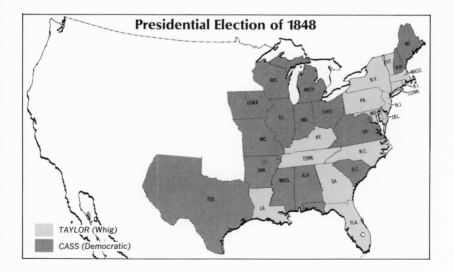

Presidential Election of 1848

TAYLOR (Whig)

CASS (Democratic)

was a situation less conducive to Northern political revolt than that of the 1850s, when the slave power seemed to take the offensive. The Free Soil movement of 1848 was therefore premature. Sectional feeling did not yet run high enough to overcome party loyalty. Nevertheless, slavery in the territories had largely superseded the old partisan issues dividing Whigs and Democrats. The existing political structure could not indefinitely withstand the great new pressures upon it.

In 1853, exactly a half century after the Louisiana purchase, a supplementary treaty with Mexico added another 45,000 square miles to the United States in exchange for $10 million. Favored by supporters of a southern railroad route to the Pacific and bitterly opposed by some antislavery leaders, this Gadsden purchase was a footnote to the record of transcontinental expansion. The spirit of manifest destiny did not then disappear, but it took the form of empty talk, like the Ostend manifesto of 1854 (asserting American claims to Cuba), or of private filibustering activities, like those of William Walker in Central America. The slavery controversy had thrown up a barrier to further acquisition of territory. More than that, the Republic had been extended about as far as possible without becoming an empire in the European fashion. The Era of Expansion was history.

Chapter VIII

Historians and the Era of Expansion

A cataclysmic event not only shapes the future but reshapes the past. One of its inevitable consequences is a radically different perspective of the era that preceded it. For example, a satisfactory history of colonial America or of the old regime in France must offer some explanation of the revolution that followed, and this requirement has often dominated the historian's selection and arrangement of data. Likewise, as any history of the United States moves forward in the nineteenth century, it becomes affected with increasing force by the climax awaiting at Fort Sumter. In written history, the Civil War extends a powerful influence backward through the preceding decades.

During the latter part of the nineteenth century, when the study of history was becoming established as a professional discipline in the United States, memories of the Civil War were still painfully fresh. The conflict had ended in victory for the opponents of slavery and in the triumph of national sovereignty over particularism. These two themes consequently assumed overwhelming importance in the treatment of Jeffersonian and Jacksonian America by writers like Hermann von Holst, James Schouler, and John W. Burgess.[1]

In such a setting, Jefferson was bound to be an ambiguous figure. A Southerner and a slaveholder, he had nevertheless been honored in antislavery rhetoric as an outspoken critic of the hated institution and as the author

---

[1] Hermann E. von Holst, *The Constitutional and Political History of the United States* (8 vols.; Chicago, 1876–1892); James Schouler, *History of the United States of America under the Constitution* (7 vols., New York, 1880–1913); John W. Burgess, *The Middle Period, 1817–1858* (New York, 1897).

of the seminal principle that all men are created equal. Jefferson's devotion to states' rights and his association with the doctrine of nullification apparently placed him on Southern ground in the sectional conflict, but this impression was at least partly counteracted by the vigorous nationalism of the Jeffersonians in power. It is therefore not surprising to find Jefferson treated favorably by Schouler, for example, and unfavorably by von Holst, even though both historians wrote with an unconcealed pro-Northern bias.

Closer to impartiality, despite the ancestry of its author, was Henry Adams' great work, *History of the United States During the Administrations of Jefferson and Madison.*[2] Adams had a sensitive understanding of the elusive, protean quality that made Jefferson's character so hard to define. Both sympathetic and critical, he saw a flawed hero who repeatedly deserted his principles under the pressure of circumstance and whose career spiraled downward in the presidency to tragicomedy and failure. The Embargo served as a perfect example of the noble purpose that has disastrous consequences. Disintegration of Jeffersonian leadership then became complete under Madison, whom Adams pictured as a weakling driven to war against his will in 1812. Yet, if the philosopher-statesmen had failed, the nation itself had met the tests of adversity. By 1815, in Adams' view, the American character and the American political system were firmly set in their democratic mold.

Few historians of the late nineteenth century tried as hard as Adams to be objective, and the general tendency of historical interpretation was anti-Jeffersonian. In many respects, Hamilton better suited the mood of urban industrial America—or at least of the intellectual elite that was writing its history. That elite, predominantly Republican and heavily concentrated in New England and New York, had begun to rehabilitate Federalism, long a term of approbrium in national politics but now winning new respect in a business-minded society. Nothing better illustrates this thrust of Republican roots into the conservative Federalist tradition than the work of the party's scholar politicians like Henry Cabot Lodge, who wrote a biography of Hamilton, and Albert J. Beveridge, who produced a masterful four-volume life of John Marshall. The revival of admiration for Hamilton meant an equivalent decline in Jefferson's reputation; for American historiography has usually treated these two men as though they were at opposite ends of a seesaw.

[2] Henry Adams, *History of the United States During the Administrations of Jefferson and Madison* (9 vols.; New York, 1889–1891).

The Jacksonians seemed even less attractive to nineteenth-century patrician historians, who might accept democracy in principle but often found it repugnant in practice. Thus von Holst and Schouler, though far apart in their estimates of Jefferson, had a common aversion for Jackson. Old Hickory, to be sure, received credit for his stalwart defense of the Union during the nullification crisis, and the laissez-faire tendencies in Jacksonian thought were appealing to social Darwinists like William Graham Sumner.[3] But historians still close to the Civil War could not forget that Jackson's party had become the stronghold of the slave power. Adopting the old abolitionist view, many of them regarded Polk's expansionism and the Mexican War as part of a general conspiracy to enlarge the domain of slavery. No less important was the patrician tendency to associate Jackson with mob rule and the vulgarization of national politics. According to this indictment, he had invented the spoils system and was thus the fountainhead of all the corruption that degraded the Gilded Age. A generation deeply concerned with civil service reform could not easily admire Andrew Jackson.

Toward the close of the century, however, a younger generation of scholars arose to challenge the judgments of their elders. During the next several decades, the balance of scholarly favor shifted decidedly toward Jefferson and Jackson. An underlying common factor was the intensified interest in American democracy that characterized the thought of the Progressive era. Furthermore, within the historical profession itself, the contemporary spirit of reform manifested itself in the determination of the new historians to remake their own discipline. They wanted to expand the scope of history beyond its traditional concern with politics and diplomacy, to associate their work with the social sciences, and to explore the connections between the past and the present. They shifted scholarly attention from institutional development to the dynamics of social change produced by environment. And since the American environment was unique, the new scholarship tended to emphasize unique rather than derivative elements in American history. By no means, however, did these younger historians speak in unison. Within the broad Progressive consensus there was considerable diversity, and the era produced several distinctive schools of historical interpretation. Unquestionably, the most influential voice was that of Frederick Jackson Turner.

Beginning in 1893 with his famous lecture on the influence of the frontier, Turner pointed to the experience of westward expansion as the primary factor

[3] William Graham Sumner, *Andrew Jackson as a Public Man* (Boston, 1882).

shaping the history of the United States. On the edge of the wilderness, he maintained, American institutions and the American character had undergone continuous change and had been pulled away from European norms. Democracy in particular had sprung from the moving frontier, which leveled away social distinctions and provided an environment of maximum freedom, individualism, and opportunity. According to Turner, it was the Western influence on Jefferson that made him the "first prophet of American democracy," and it was as the "very personification" of frontier democracy that Jackson became the nation's first popular hero. Turner's hypothesis, fitting the whole national experience into a single organic process, thus offered a comprehensive explanation of why America was different from Europe and why Americans were like one another. Later, he added a sectional explanation of differentiation and conflict in American life, but here again it was the ever-changing West that played the dynamic and decisive role.[4]

New college courses and a growing output of books on the westward movement marked the emergence of an enthusiastic Turner school in American historical scholarship. Yet much of its work was done by men of narrower vision who often seemed to forget that Turner's interest centered less on the West itself than on the intricate connections between westward expansion and national development. A more subtle indication of his profound influence is the degree to which the Turner outlook gradually permeated general American history and especially the history of the first half of the nineteenth century. Although he gave some attention to earlier and later frontiers, Turner's own studies dealt primarily with the settlement of the Mississippi Valley and with the patterns of sectionalism that took shape between 1815 and 1850. His generalizations, in turn, had their maximum effect upon interpretations of this same period—the Era of Expansion.[5]

A notable example is the shift of emphasis in the explanation of why the nation went to war in 1812. The conventional interpretation had followed Madison's war message in stressing maritime factors, particularly British blockade and impressment policies. But this scarcely accounted for the belligerence of the West and the role of the War Hawks. The newer view

[4] Frederick Jackson Turner, *The Frontier in American History* (New York, 1920); *The Significance of Sections in American History* (New York, 1932).

[5] Frederick Jackson Turner, *Rise of the New West, 1819–1829* (New York, 1906); *The United States, 1830–1850* (New York, 1935).

that gained wide acceptance in the 1920s explained the war as a manifestation of Western expansionism. According to one historian, the frontiersman's insatiable hunger for land was translated into a determination to conquer Canada. Another insisted that Westerners wanted American annexation of Canada and Florida in order to eliminate the Indian menace on the northern and southern borders. The latter explanation carried greater conviction, but both were within the Turner tradition.[6]

Meanwhile, other historians had elaborated the Turner interpretation of Jacksonian Democracy as a triumph of Western leadership and Western values. Although there were still misgivings about Jackson's influence upon the quality of American politics, he was now generally praised for putting Jeffersonian principles to work and advancing the cause of popular government.[7] One important book struck directly at the old patrician complaint about spoilsmanship by demonstrating that patronage was essential to the functioning of the party system.[8] It reflected a growing scholarly appreciation of political parties as the machinery of democracy that helped place the Jacksonians in a more favorable light. At the same time, Polk and the expansionists of the 1840s were rescued from the old abolitionist interpretation and made the spokesmen for an army of pioneers marching irresistibly westward to the Pacific. The overseas imperialism of 1898 also affected the climate of historical opinion. In Justin H. Smith's monumental study of the Mexican War, American policy was defended at almost every turn.[9]

To some extent, the frontier thesis diverted attention from the slavery controversy, which had so dominated the writings of earlier historians like von Holst. Turner did not belittle the issue, but he insisted that it must be fitted into a more complex pattern of sectional conflict. In any case, said Turner, the slavery controversy resolved itself into a struggle for control of the West, which became the focus of each major crisis between North and South. Thus it was the issue of slavery together with the process of westward expansion that proved to be the explosive combination. Such a

[6] Louis M Hacker, "Western Land Hunger and the War of 1812," *Mississippi Valley Historical Review*, Vol. X (March, 1924); Julius W. Pratt, *Expansionists of 1812* (New York, 1925).

[7] William MacDonald, *Jacksonian Democracy, 1828–1837* (New York, 1907); William E. Dodd, *Expansion and Conflict* (Boston, 1915); John Spencer Bassett, *The Life of Andrew Jackson* (2 vols.; Garden City, N.Y., 1911).

[8] Carl Russell Fish, *The Civil Service and the Patronage* (New York, 1905).

[9] Justin H. Smith, *The War with Mexico* (2 vols.; New York, 1919).

perspective tended to incorporate even the coming of the Civil War into the frontier hypothesis. It scaled down the moral and constitutional aspects of the slavery question, emphasizing instead a kind of competition for empire in which two sections of the Union assumed the roles once played by European powers. When historians came to explain the Kansas-Nebraska Act as the consequence, primarily, of sectional rivalry over the location of a transcontinental railroad, they were following a course already marked out by Turner.[10]

Conflict, in Turner's synthesis, remained subordinate to a larger organic process—the unfolding of American institutions under the influence of the westward movement. For Charles A. Beard, on the other hand, conflict between shifting social classes and interest groups was the central theme of American history. Progressive imperatives mingled with Marxian currents from abroad in Beard's line of thought, which led him, essentially, to economic motivation as the determinant of political behavior. Applying it first in his famous work on the Constitution, he subsequently extended this economic interpretation to Jeffersonian and Jacksonian democracy.[11] The election of 1800, he said, meant the triumph of the agrarian masses led by a slaveholding aristocracy against Hamiltonian capitalism. But not until the Jacksonians added urban workers to the democratic coalition did political alignments reflect the fundamental divisions of an emerging industrial society. Beard, like Turner, saw in Andrew Jackson a symbolic figure of paramount importance—not the representative frontiersman, however, but rather "gladiator-at-large" for the common people in their struggles with the "moneyed classes."

The economic interpretation of American history, commonly attributed to Beard, but actually advancing on a broad front of scholarship, became especially influential during the two decades following World War I. Its relationship to Turner's sectional approach is not easily defined. In some degree, the two schools were complementary. Beard acknowledged that class interests in the nineteenth century were frequently sectionalized, while Turner defined sections as "natural economic groupings" and often seemed close to economic determinism. It is significant, for example, that a number of

[10] Frank H. Hodder, "The Railroad Background of the Kansas-Nebraska Act," *Mississippi Valley Historical Review*, Vol. XII (June, 1925).

[11] Charles A. Beard, *Economic Origins of Jeffersonian Democracy* (New York, 1915); Charles A. and Mary R. Beard, *The Rise of American Civilization* (2 vols.; New York, 1927).

studies examining the economic bases of Southern sectionalism owed more to Turner than to Beard.[12] Both historians emphasized materialistic sources of human action, and both tended to by-pass the moral conflict inherent in the slavery question. At the same time, Beard and other writers of similar outlook could not accept the frontier hypothesis with its rhapsodic pronouncements on the dominating influence of free land in American history. Turner, they insisted, had largely ignored the most dynamic factor of all—the rise of industrial capitalism, together with the urban social order and the class conflict that industrialization produced. Here was one prong of a general attack soon to be launched against the whole Turner tradition.[13]

Still another strand of Progressive history blended with the formulations of Turner and Beard but also embodied a potential challenge to their materialsim. Vernon Louis Parrington's *Main Currents in American Thought* was the work of a latter-day Jeffersonian whose nostalgic affection for the old agricultural republic led him into disillusionment with the industrial society that had replaced it.[14] Jefferson is so much the central pivot in this first great intellectual history of the American people, that it might well have been titled "The Rise and Decline of Jeffersonian Democracy." Parrington traced Jefferson's liberal idealism to French and English sources, his egalitarian tendencies to the influence of the frontier. Jackson, in *Main Currents,* is a representative Westerner and thus an "agrarian liberal" disposed to preserve the simple, decentralized political and social order that Jefferson had idealized. The great weakness of Jacksonian Democracy was that it relied upon the accumulated fund of Jeffersonian ideas and developed no new philosophy to meet the onrush of acquisitive capitalism. With the age of Jackson, in Parrington's view, there began the tragic erosion of Jeffersonian liberalism, but it was the "fault of the times," rather than of Old Hickory.

---

[12] Robert R. Russel, *Economic Aspects of Southern Sectionalism, 1840–1861* (New York, 1924); John G. Van Deusen, *Economic Bases of Disunion in South Carolina* (New York, 1928); Avery O. Craven, *Soil Exhaustion as a Factor in the Agricultural History of Virginia and Maryland, 1606–1860* (Urbana, Ill., 1926).

[13] Charles A. Beard, "The Frontier in American History," *New Republic,* Vol. XXV (February 16, 1921). Evaluations of the Turner hypothesis have been collected in George Rogers Taylor, ed., *The Turner Thesis* (Boston, 1949); O. Lawrence Burnette, Jr., ed., *Wisconsin Witness to Frederick Jackson Turner* (Madison, 1961); Ray Allen Billington, ed., *The Frontier Thesis* (New York, 1966).

[14] Vernon Louis Parrington, *Main Currents in American Thought* (3 vols.; New York, 1927, 1930).

However much he adopted of the Turner hypothesis, Parrington was even closer to the economic determinism of Beard, taking as his major theme the everlasting conflict between the Hamiltonian and Jeffersonian visions of America. Yet the success of *Main Currents* helped inspire an enthusiasm for intellectual history that not even Beard could resist. No doubt the challenge of totalitarian ideologies in the 1930s also promoted investigation of the ideas and commitments that constituted the "American spirit." And ideas taken seriously are bound to limit the force of determinism and materialism. A case in point is Ralph Henry Gabriel's *The Course of American Democratic Thought,* a study of the concepts and beliefs clustering in the persistent democratic faith of the nineteenth century. According to Gabriel, this "secular national religion" had already been firmly established by 1815, and its doctrinal foundation was a threefold belief in a moral order, the free individual, and the mission of America.[15]

Despite the mounting prestige of intellectual history, however, it did not produce a revolution in the interpretation of the American past. More often than not, historians continued to treat ideas as superstructure resting upon economic and other "realistic" motives. For example, Albert K. Weinberg's exhaustive effort to catalog all of the concepts associated with "manifest destiny" proved to be largely a study of rationalization rather than motivation.[16] The vogue of intellectual history, moreover, encouraged a shift of attention to those Eastern urban centers where the most important ideas originated. In this respect, it tended to support the Beardian rejection of the frontier hypothesis. Turner himself became a subject of considerable interest for intellectual historians, but only in a few special ways were they willing to follow him into the West.

On the eve of World War II, the Progressive view of American history still generally prevailed in classrooms and textbooks, though significant changes were already evident on the frontiers of scholarship. The Great Depression sharpened interest in economic interpretation, and the New Deal years provided a congenial setting for the theme of democracy battling against privilege. Even the Turner thesis, precisely because it did not fit twentieth-century America, served to justify new departures in public policy. Keynsian economic thought of the 1930s, as applied to the United States, rested squarely upon the assumption that some equivalent must be found for the

[15] Ralph Henry Gabriel, *The Course of American Democratic Thought* (New York, 1940).
[16] Albert K. Weinberg, *Manifest Destiny* (Baltimore, 1935).

dynamic influence of the frontier, now no longer operative. Criticism of Turner was mounting, it is true, but his ideas had not yet lost their momentum. Turner students, many of them now prominent historians, carried on the tradition, extending and modifying it as they went. William Warren Sweet's numerous studies of American Protestantism, stressing the democratizing effects of westward expansion, exemplify the persisting vitality of the frontier hypothesis.[17]

Democratic ascendancy in national politics after 1932 tended to exalt the party's great heroes of the past, especially since the New Deal period apparently made Democrats of American historians in overwhelming numbers. Jefferson in particular was a center of attention, partly because the bicentenary of his birth was near, and work had begun on the Memorial building in Washington, D.C., but also because of his relevance in contemporary political and social controversy. Was the New Deal a fulfillment or a betrayal of the Jeffersonian tradition? Many voices echoed the words of Charles M. Wiltse, who argued that the policies of Franklin D. Roosevelt were "essentially Jeffersonian," though admittedly on the "social rather than the individualistic side of the tradition." Yet Jefferson's rhetoric also lent itself easily to use by opponents of federal power, and some Republican leaders claimed him as a patron saint of their party, indeed, as the ultimate alternative to Marx. Somewhat apart from the political battle, there were men like the twelve Southern authors of *I'll Take My Stand* who joined Parrington in viewing Jefferson as the symbol of lost values and a shattered dream.[18]

Although Jeffersonian scholarship continued to flourish after 1945,[19] it was Jacksonian Democracy that became a primary focus of historical study and controversy. The new phase began with the publication of *The Age of Jackson,* by Arthur M. Schlesinger, Jr., a transitional book that also proved to be seminal. Schlesinger aligned himself emphatically with Progressive historians of the Beard variety, rejecting the Western interpretation and insisting that Jacksonian Democracy was a problem of classes rather than

[17] William Warren Sweet, *The Story of Religion in America* (New York, 1930); *Revivalism in America* (New York, 1944).

[18] Charles M. Wiltse, *The Jeffersonian Tradition in American Democracy* (Chapel Hill, N.C., 1935); Twelve Southerners, *I'll Take My Stand* (New York, 1930).

[19] Notably Dumas Malone's work in progress, *Jefferson and His Time* (3 vols.; Boston, 1948–; Irving Brant, *James Madison* (6 vols.; Indianapolis, 1941–1961); Merrill D. Peterson, *The Jefferson Image in the American Mind* (New York, 1960).

sections. Eastern cities, in his view, were the true sources of the movement, and the workingmen of those cities played the most crucial role. Jackson and his followers, despite their Jeffersonian commitments, were compelled to use governmental power for the protection of farmers, laborers, and other lesser folk against the increasing exploitation and political influence of the business community. Thus Schlesinger connected Jacksonianism with positive government in such a way as to make it virtually an ancestor of the New Deal.[20]

With the Schlesinger book, Jackson's reputation reached its peak. A poll of leading historians in 1948 ranked him among the six "great" presidents. But to this highly favorable judgment Thomas P. Abernethy had already entered a strong dissent by portraying Jackson in Tennessee politics as a frontier aristocrat who displayed little interest in the common people and made a demagogue's use of democratic appeals. Charles M. Wiltse, in his impressive biography of Calhoun, was equally hostile to Jackson, whom he labeled a "frontier bully."[21] Other historians attacked Schlesinger's "labor thesis," pointing out that Jackson appeared unsympathetic to unions and strikers, that the Jacksonians by no means won the full support of laboring men, and that the workingmen's movements of the time were essentially bourgeois rather than proletarian in nature.[22]

Furthermore, said one group of Schlesinger's critics, the Jacksonian movement was not antagonistic to business enterprise. On the contrary, it embodied the aggressive spirit of capitalism and aimed only at opening the avenues of enterprise to all Americans by eliminating monopoly and other forms of special privilege. This "entrepreneurial" interpretation, advanced by such historians as Richard Hofstadter and Bray Hammond, had the effect of blurring the difference between Whig and Democrat, while emphasizing the "common climate" of public opinion.[23] The question of whether partisan loyalties reflected significant class and doctrinal cleavages

[20] Arthur M. Schlesinger, Jr., *The Age of Jackson* (Boston, 1945).

[21] Thomas P. Abernethy, *From Frontier to Plantation in Tennessee* (Chapel Hill, N.C., 1932); Charles M. Wiltse, *John C. Calhoun* (3 vols.; Indianapolis, 1944–1951).

[22] Richard B. Morris, "Andrew Jackson, Strikebreaker," *American Historical Review*, Vol. LV (October, 1949); Edward Pessen, "The Workingmen's Movement of the Jacksonian Era," *Mississippi Valley Historical Review*, Vol. XLIII (December, 1956); Walter Hugins, *Jacksonian Democracy and the Working Class* (Stanford, Calif., 1960).

[23] Richard Hofstadter, *The American Political Tradition* (New York, 1948); Bray Hammond, *Banks and Politics in America* (Princeton, N.J., 1957).

received careful attention in a number of monographs on state politics. The results varied, but negative answers predominated.[24] Likewise, Charles S. Sydnor concluded that Southern voters generally were "unable to see much difference between Whigs and Democrats." On the other hand, Glyndon G. Van Deusen in a survey of the whole Jacksonian era declared that the Whigs were more conservative and closer to the business community, that the Democrats were more liberal and more responsive to the aspirations of the common man. Yet Van Deusen also added that by 1848, "it was difficult to distinguish between the national principles of Whiggery and Democracy."[25]

Contributing to the same effect was the influence of behavioral science in new studies of the American party system. Such scholarship concentrated upon the developing structure and function of political organizations as more or less independent entities with their own internal purposes and controls. Viewed from this angle, the primary task of a political party was to win elections, rather than to promote a set of doctrines, effectuate a program, or satisfy outside interests. The behavioral approach thus had some tendency to incapsulate the party system, and at the same time it stressed the institutional behavior common to all parties. Anticipated in certain respects by several earlier writers like Mosei Ostrogorski, it is admirably exemplified in Richard P. McCormick's study of party formation during the Jacksonian era. Apparently conceding that fundamental issues played some part in the emergence of the Federalist and Republican organizations during the 1790s, McCormick stated flatly that the "second American party system" was formed and maintained "essentially for the purpose of contesting for the presidency." From 1824 to 1840, this "presidential question," instead of doctrinal dispute, was "the axis around which politics revolved."[26]

One local study deserving special attention because of its wide influence is Lee Benson's study of Jacksonian politics in New York. There, according to Benson, the Democrats were actually the conservative party, not only

---

[24] Paul Murray, *The Whig Party in Georgia, 1825–1853* (Chapel Hill, N.C., 1948); William S. Hoffman, *Andrew Jackson and North Carolina Politics* (Chapel Hill, N.C., 1958); Herbert J. Doherty, *The Whigs of Florida* (Gainesville, Fla., 1959); Edwin A. Miles, *Jacksonian Democracy in Mississippi* (Chapel Hill, N.C., 1960); Arthur W. Thompson, *Jacksonian Democracy on the Florida Frontier* (Gainesville, Fla., 1961).

[25] Charles S. Sydnor, *The Development of Southern Sectionalism, 1819–1848* (Baton Rouge, La., 1948); Glyndon G. Van Deusen, *The Jacksonian Era* (New York, 1959).

[26] Richard P. McCormick, *The Second American Party System* (Chapel Hill, N.C., 1966).

slower than Whigs and Anti-Masons to embrace egalitarian principles but persistently hostile to state programs aimed at humanitarian reform. In addition, his analysis of election statistics led Benson to deny that economic differences governed political alignments. Other factors, especially ethnic and religious ties, more distinctly affected voting behavior. The whole concept of Jacksonian Democracy, Benson concluded, was such a distortion of historical realities that it ought to be discarded.[27]

Meanwhile, two other historians had examined Jacksonian rhetoric in a search for the essential temper and emotional appeal of the movement. John William Ward found that Jackson was made to symbolize the natural strength and wisdom, as well as the providential destiny, of the postfrontier Western farmer, neatly poised between the savagery of the wilderness and the corruption of older civilizations. As such, the Jacksonian image celebrated a social order that was already "slipping away." Marvin Meyers laid even heavier stress upon the uneasy ambivalence with which Jacksonian Americans viewed their rapidly changing world. While plunging forward in the rush of speculative enterprise, they looked backward and yearned for the simple virtues of the "Old Republic." The Democrats, said Meyers, spoke principally to the fears and resentments of the people; it was the Whigs who "affirmed the material promise of American life."[28]

These new patterns of Jacksonian scholarship reflect certain trends in American historiography as a whole. The intellectual historian, for example, has extended his investigations far beyond formal writings of the intellectual class to the diffuse, misty realm of popular belief, emotional response, and social symbols. Such is the case with Oscar Handlin's *The Uprooted,* a sensitive effort to explain the "shock of alienation" suffered by immigrants cut off from the familiar culture of their ancestors and clinging precariously to the social fringes of the strange new world. The dynamic influence of cultural myth upon historical action has received particular attention. Just as Ward examined the symbolic Jackson who existed only in minds hungry for reassurance, so William R. Taylor studied the manufacture of the cavalier myth by Southerners seeking to quarantine their section from Yankee contamination. These and other inquiries owed much to the example of Henry Nash Smith's pioneering work, *Virgin Land: The American West as*

---

[27] Lee Benson, *The Concept of Jacksonian Democracy* (Princeton, N.J., 1961).

[28] John William Ward, *Andrew Jackson: Symbol for an Age* (New York, 1953); Marvin Meyers, *The Jacksonian Persuasion* (Stanford, Calif., 1957).

Symbol and Myth. The most important of its several themes was the development of a concept that proved to be more powerful than reality—the West idealized as the "Garden of the World," where a beneficent nature rewarded agricultural virtues, and American society was constantly bathed in waters of rejuvenation.[29]

As for economic interpretation, it retained much of its vitality in the newer Jacksonian scholarship. There were dissenters like Benson, to be sure, and like William W. Freehling, who argued persuasively that the nullification movement in South Carolina was inspired more by fears concerning slavery than by financial distress.[30] But Beard's emphasis upon economic determinants of political behavior, though modified, has not been repudiated. The fascination of the Jacksonian period results in no small part from the fact that this was really the first generation of Americans to face the implications of the industrial revolution. Indeed, historians and economists have found the whole first half of the nineteenth century to be a rewarding field for the study of economic change, and their investigations have become increasingly sophisticated and precise. One group of monographs, for instance, examined the role of state government in economic development before the Civil War, and while doing so they very nearly dissolved the myth of a golden age of laissez-faire. To some extent, these works reversed the Beardian order of things by presenting a political interpretation of economic history.[31]

What did lose ground decidedly was the theme of class conflict that had pervaded the writings of Beard and Schlesinger. Their critics discovered greater complexity and yet an underlying unity in Jacksonian America. The record revealed too much division within economic interest groups, too many exceptions and contradictions and shiftings and variations to fit the simple picture of masses versus classes. At the same time, a number of

---

[29] Oscar Handlin, *The Uprooted* (Boston, 1951); William R. Taylor, *Cavalier and Yankee* (New York, 1961); Henry Nash Smith, *Virgin Land: The American West as Symbol and Myth* (Cambridge, Mass., 1950).

[30] William W. Freehling, *Prelude to Civil War: The Nullification Controversy in South Carolina, 1816–1836* (New York, 1965).

[31] Oscar and Mary Flug Handlin, *Commonwealth, A Study of the Role of Government in the American Economy: Massachusetts, 1774–1861* (New York, 1947); Louis Hartz, *Economic Policy and Democratic Thought: Pennsylvania, 1776–1860* (Cambridge, Mass., 1948); James N. Primm, *Economic Policy in the Development of a Western State: Missouri, 1820–1860* (Cambridge, Mass., 1954).

historians had reached the conclusion that class and partisan differences were less significant than the degree to which most Americans shared a common set of values. Both Jacksonians and anti-Jacksonians, they asserted, openly embraced the democratic faith, played the same game of politics, and responded vigorously to the lure of acquisitive capitalism.

This tendency to stress consensus, instead of dualism and conflict, extended into other periods of American history. In three general studies published almost simultaneously, Louis Hartz found that all Americans were the heirs, and to some extent the prisoners, of the same "liberal tradition"; Daniel Boorstin celebrated their consistent preference for pragmatic achievement, unencumbered by systematic philosophy; and David M. Potter examined the common experience of economic abundance as a distinctive influence on the formation of national character.[32] Where antagonism plainly existed, its causes were now often internalized by scholars acquainted with the insights of psychology. A social agitator might seem preoccupied with objective evil, but the motive agent was identified as a gnawing personal anxiety. The abolitionists, according to David Donald, were sons and daughters of established families who suffered from a decline of status and a feeling of alienation in the new entrepreneurial society. Southern slave-holders, argued Charles G. Sellers, reacted violently to Northern criticism because of their concealed struggle with an agonizing sense of guilt.[33]

The great crusade for Negro rights that began during the 1950s brought renewed interest in earlier phases of the struggle and an outpouring of scholarship from historians who were themselves often intensely and actively committed to the cause. This development seemed likely to produce a sizable rip in the fabric of consensus by restoring to its former prominence the theme of moral conflict over slavery. Such was not precisely the case, however, even though sympathetic treatment of the abolitionists did become fashion-able again. The new writers were concerned not only with the subject of slavery but with the Negro as a human being and the whole pattern of racial attitudes in the United States. They demonstrated that Northerners, except for a tiny saving remnant, more or less shared the Southern belief

---

[32] Louis Hartz, *The Liberal Tradition in America* (New York, 1955); Daniel J. Boorstin, *The Genius of American Politics* (Chicago, 1953); David M. Potter, *People of Plenty* (Chicago, 1954).

[33] David Donald, *Lincoln Reconsidered* (New York, 1956); Charles Grier Sellers, Jr., ed., *The Southerner as American* (Chapel Hill, N.C., 1960).

in white supremacy, that segregation and other forms of discrimination actually increased in the free states during the years of the antislavery campaign. Thus, beneath the sectional conflict over slavery, they discovered a national consensus that explained why the Emancipation Proclamation did not make the Negro free.[34]

The newer writings on Jacksonian Democracy were also representative of a general historiographical trend in their tendency to discount the Turner hypothesis. Both Schlesinger and his critics presented Eastern, urban interpretations that gave little weight to the influence of the frontier. Other scholars saw the West primarily as a source of democratic symbols used for manipulative purposes. The way had been prepared for an anti-Turner cycle by mounting criticism in the 1930s, but its full effect did not become apparent until after World War II. At first, the reaction took the form of essays severely appraising Turner's own writings. He was charged with impreciseness and overstatement; with neglecting important factors like technology and immigration; with attributing contradictory qualities, such as idealism and materialism, to the influence of the frontier; and with visualizing the West as both a paradise and a purgatory. A special target was Turner's repeated assertion that "the rise of democracy. . . meant the triumph of the frontier." His critics pointed to the European origins of democratic theory and to the fact that Eastern states were often ahead of the West in adopting democratic practices. But the attack fell most heavily upon Turner's suggestion that Western lands, by draining off discontented workers, reduced social pressures in the East. Investigation revealed that this "safety valve" did not work when it was needed. Urban laborers seldom possessed the necessary money and skill to become pioneer farmers; westward migration declined during times of economic depression; and eventually it was the cities that operated as a safety valve for rural discontent.[35]

Although other historians were soon at work defending the frontier thesis or at least trying to salvage it in part, there was a definite ebbing of Turner's influence on American historical writing. This "decline of the West," so pronounced in Jacksonian scholarship, shortly became evident elsewhere. For example, the frontier no longer dominated explanations of why the

---

[34] Leon F. Litwack, *North of Slavery* (Chicago, 1961); Martin Duberman, ed., *The Anti-Slavery Vanguard* (Princeton, N.J., 1965).

[35] Criticism of Turner is summarized in Ray Allen Billington, *The American Frontier* (2nd ed.; Washington, 1965); *America's Frontier Heritage* (New York, 1966).

United States went to war in 1812. The emphasis swung back to maritime issues once more, but with particular stress upon the intense feeling in all sections of the country that the national honor, repeatedly outraged, had to be defended. The great outcry for conquest of Canada, said one scholar, sprang primarily from the desire to strike the enemy in his most vulnerable spot. Meanwhile Norman A. Graebner had advanced a maritime interpretation of Polk's expansionist program, which was inspired, he maintained, more by the mercantile desire for Pacific seaports than by pressure from Western pioneers or the spirit of manifest destiny. In a later study, Frederick Merk concluded that manifest destiny, unlike the much loftier concept of American mission, had never been a true expression of the national spirit.[36]

By the 1960s, even though Western history still poured off the presses and remained a standard subject in colleges and universities, the Turner tradition had plainly lost most of its steam and much of its prestige. Of course it was equally plain that Turner had not been entirely wrong, since the occupation of a continent must have had *some* effect upon the structure and quality of American civilization. Yet the effort to save his hypothesis by pruning away all the excesses and defects attributed to it could only convert a challenging overstatement into a sterile truism. More promising was the concurrent tendency to liberate the frontier from its conceptual isolation and integrate it with other historical forces in new explanatory arrangements.

Such assimilation of the Turner thesis began in the 1950s. Perhaps the best illustration is Potter's study of abundance, which he ascribed to the natural wealth of the West and the cultural achievements of technology, each interacting with the other. Viewed in this way, the exhaustion of the public domain seemed less cataclysmic than Turner had pictured it, since the slack was taken up by accelerated technological change. Thus Potter's formulation, unlike Turner's, included the twentieth century in its compass. At the same time, Hartz attributed the American liberal consensus to the absence of a feudal tradition, which in turn resulted from the prevalence of Lockean theory and the abundance of land. Thus Turner, according to Hartz, was actually "half right." Still another historian, Rowland Berthoff,

[36] Reginald Horsman, *The Causes of the War of 1812* (New York, 1962); Bradford Perkins, ed., *The Causes of the War of 1812; National Honor or National Interest* (New York, 1962); Norman A Graebner, *Empire on the Pacific* (New York, 1955); Frederick Merk, *Manifest Destiny and Mission in American History* (New York, 1963).

suggested that what made the nineteenth century unique was the extreme mobility of the American people and the consequent disorganization of the social order. Westward expansion, he declared, was obviously one of the major mass movements and a leveling force of prime importance, but it had to be associated with other kinds of internal migration, with the waves of immigration, and with the social mobility that accompanied industrialization.[37]

These and other writings indicate that the behavioral emphasis upon greater precision has not dimmed the historian's hope of finding some logical core or ruling principle in his assembled data. With several thousand scholars now at work in the field of American history, the proliferation of fresh discoveries, of new theses and newer antitheses, almost defies orderly survey and makes any summary, such as this one, quickly obsolescent. Interpretation of the Era of Expansion may still be in its infancy. The period contains so many roots of contemporary America that it will not soon tire the historian's interest.

[37] Rowland Berthoff, "The American Social Order: A Conservative Hypothesis," *American Historical Review,* Vol. LXV (April, 1960).

Some Books for Further Reading

The date of first publication is given. An asterisk indicates that there is a paperback edition.

Bakeless, John. *Lewis and Clark* (1947).*

Barnhart, John D. *Valley of Democracy* (1953).

Benson, Lee. *The Concept of Jacksonian Democracy* (1961).*

Billington, Ray A. *The Far Western Frontier* (1956).*

——————. *America's Frontier Heritage* (1966).*

——————. *The Protestant Crusade* (1938).*

Boorstin, Daniel J. *The Americans: The National Experience* (1965).*

Caruso, John A. *The Great Lakes Frontier* (1960).

Cash, W.J. *The Mind of the South* (1941).*

Coles, Harry C. *The War of 1812* (1965).*

Cunningham, Noble E. *The Jeffersonian Republicans in Power* (1963).*

Dana, Richard Henry. *Two Years Before the Mast* (1840).*

Dangerfield, George. *The Awakening of American Nationalism* (1965).*

Dick, Everett. *The Dixie Frontier* (1948).*

Eaton, Clement. *The Growth of Southern Civilization* (1961).*

Filler, Louis. *The Crusade Against Slavery* (1960).*

Fischer, David H. *The Revolution of American Conservatism* (1965).

Fishlow, Alfred. *American Railroads and the Transformation of the Antebellum Economy* (1965).

Freehling, William W. *Prelude to Civil War* (1966).*

Gates, Paul W. *The Farmer's Age* (1960).

Graebner, Norman A. *Empire on the Pacific* (1955).

Green, Constance M. *Eli Whitney and the Birth of American Technology* (1956).*

Hammond, Bray. *Banks and Politics in America* (1957).*

Handlin, Oscar and Mary F. *Commonwealth: A Study of the Role of Government in the American Economy* (1947).

Jones, Maldwyn A. *American Immigration* (1960).*

Larkin, Oliver W. *Art and Life in America* (1949).

Litwack, Leon. *North of Slavery* (1961).*

McCormick, Richard P. *The Second American Party System* (1966).*

Marx, Leo. *The Machine in the Garden* (1964).*

Merk, Frederick. *Manifest Destiny and Mission* (1963).*

Meyers, Marvin. *The Jacksonian Persuasion* (1957).*

Miller, Douglas T. *Jacksonian Aristocracy* (1967).

Moore, Glover. *The Missouri Controversy* (1953).*

Nye, Russel B. *The Cultural Life of the New Nation* (1960).*

Parkman, Francis. *The Oregon Trail* (1849).*

Parrington, Vernon L. *The Romantic Revolution in America* (1927).*

Paul, James C.N. *Rift in the Democracy* (1951).*

Peterson, Merrill. *The Jefferson Image in American Thought* (1960).*

Poage, George R. *Henry Clay and the Whig Party* (1936).

Remini, Robert V. *The Election of Andrew Jackson* (1963).*

Schlesinger, Arthur M., Jr. *The Age of Jackson* (1945).*

Sellers, Charles. *James K. Polk, Continentalist* (1966).

Smith, Henry Nash. *Virgin Land* (1950).*

Spencer, Benjamin T., *The Quest for Nationality* (1957).

Stampp, Kenneth M. *The Peculiar Institution* (1956).*

Stegner, Wallace. *The Gathering of Zion* (1964).

Sydnor, Charles S. *The Development of Southern Sectionalism* (1948).

Taylor, George R. *The Transportation Revolution* (1951).*

Taylor, William R. *Cavalier and Yankee* (1961).*

Tocqueville, Alexis de. *Democracy in America* (1835–40).*

Turner, Frederick Jackson. *The Rise of the New West* (1906).*

Tyler, Alice Felt. *Freedom's Ferment* (1944).*

Van Deusen, Glyndon G. *The Jacksonian Era* (1959).*

Van Every, Dale. *Disinherited: The Lost Birthright of the American Indian* (1966).*

Wade, Richard C. *The Urban Frontier* (1959).*

Illustration Credits

Index

DATE DUE

DEMCO 38-297